Eine Arbeitsgemeinschaft der Verlage

Böhlau Verlag · Wien · Köln · Weimar
Verlag Barbara Budrich · Opladen · Farmington Hills
facultas.wuv · Wien
Wilhelm Fink · München
A. Francke Verlag · Tübingen und Basel
Haupt Verlag · Bern · Stuttgart · Wien
Julius Klinkhardt Verlagsbuchhandlung · Bad Heilbrunn
Mohr Siebeck · Tübingen
Nomos Verlagsgesellschaft · Baden-Baden
Orell Füssli Verlag · Zürich
Ernst Reinhardt Verlag · München · Basel
Ferdinand Schöningh · Paderborn · München · Wien · Zürich
Eugen Ulmer Verlag · Stuttgart
UVK Verlagsgesellschaft · Konstanz, mit UVK/Lucius · München
Vandenhoeck & Ruprecht · Göttingen
vdf Hochschulverlag AG an der ETH Zürich

StandardWissen Lehramt

Die Bände zur Didaktik des Englischen werden herausgegeben
von Engelbert Thaler

Bislang sind erschienen in der Reihe:

Teaching Grammar von J.-U. Keßler/A. Plesser (UTB 3448)
Task-Supported Language Learning von A. Müller-Hartmann/
M. Schocker-von Ditfurth (UTB 3336)
Teaching English Literature von E. Thaler (UTB 2897)
Computer-assisted Language Learning von K. Heim/M. Ritter (UTB 3334)

Katja Heim / Markus Ritter

Teaching English:
Computer-assisted Language Learning

Ferdinand Schöningh

Die Autoren:

Markus Ritter is a Professor of Teaching English as a Foreign Language (TEFL) at the Ruhr-Universität Bochum, Germany. He is an author of various educational multimedia programs, most notably the English Coach software series for the secondary sector in Germany. His special interests lie in future perspectives of electronic media in language learning and new approaches to teacher training.

Katja Heim is a lecturer for Teaching English as a Foreign Language (TEFL) at the University of Duisburg-Essen, Germany. She is an author of educational software and has done advisory work for publishing houses and an online language school. Her research interests are the natural integration of media into English lessons, how to foster learners' autonomy as well as future perspectives of primary English teaching.

Online-Angebote oder elektronische Ausgaben sind erhältlich unter **www.utb-shop.de**

Bibliografische Information der Deutschen Nationalbibliothek

Die Deutsche Nationalbibliothek verzeichnet diese Publikation in der Deutschen Nationalbibliografie; detaillierte bibliografische Daten sind im Internet über http://dnb.d-nb.de abrufbar.

© 2012 Ferdinand Schöningh, Paderborn
(Verlag Ferdinand Schöningh GmbH & Co. KG, Jühenplatz 1, D-33098 Paderborn)

Internet: www.schoeningh.de

Printed in Germany.
Herstellung: Ferdinand Schöningh, Paderborn
Einbandgestaltung: Atelier Reichert, Stuttgart

UTB-Band-Nr: 3334
ISBN 978-3-8252-3334-1

Vorwort zur Reihe

StandardWissen Lehramt – Studienbücher für die Praxis

Wie das gesamte Bildungswesen wird sich auch die künftige Lehr-
amtsausbildung an Kompetenzen und Standards orientieren.
Damit rückt die Frage in den Vordergrund, was Lehrkräfte wissen
und können müssen, um ihre berufliche Praxis erfolgreich zu
bewältigen. Das Spektrum reicht von fachlichen Fähigkeiten über
Diagnosekompetenzen bis hin zu pädagogisch-psychologischem
Wissen, um Lehren als Unterstützung zur Selbsthilfe und Lernen
als eigenaktiven Prozess fassen zu können.

Kompetenzen werden nicht in einem Zug erworben; Lehrerbil-
dung umfasst nicht nur das Studium an einer Hochschule, sondern
ebenso das Referendariat und die Berufsphase. Die Reihe StandardWissen Lehramt bei UTB bietet daher Lehramtsstudierenden,
Referendaren, Lehrern in der Berufseinstiegsphase und Fortbil-
dungsteilnehmern jenes wissenschaftlich abgesicherte Know-
How, das sie im Rahmen einer neu orientierten Ausbildung wie
auch später in der Schule benötigen. Fachdidaktische und päda-
gogisch-psychologische Themen werden gleichermaßen in dieser
Buchreihe vertreten sein – einer Basisbibliothek für alle Lehramtsstudierenden, Referendare, Lehrerinnen und Lehrer.

FOR UWE, MAX AND VERA

Table of Contents

1. **BASIS** 9
   1.1 Why a book on computers in the language classroom? 10
   1.2 Computers in the language classroom – a brief historical overview . . . 11
   1.3 Structuring the field of CALL – and this book 16

2. **WRITTEN ONLINE COMMUNICATION** 19
   2.1 Overview 20
   2.2 Chat 21
   2.3 E-mail 23
   2.4 Forums, discussion boards, bulletin boards 27
   2.5 Focus on research 29
   2.6 Classroom ideas 32

3. **ORAL ONLINE COMMUNICATION** 35
   3.1 Overview 36
   3.2 Synchronous oral communication 36
   3.3 Asynchronous oral communication 37
   3.4 Focus on research 40
   3.5 Classroom ideas 43

4. **WEB RESOURCES** 47
   4.1 Overview 48
   4.2 Web and Internet: a brief definition of terms 48
   4.3 Web Portals 49
   4.4 Reference Tools 58
   4.5 Focus on research 67
   4.6 Classroom ideas 68

5. **WEB RESEARCH** 74
   5.1 Overview 74
   5.2 Webquests 74
   5.3 Search Enginges 81
   5.4 Focus on Research 90
   5.5 Classroom Ideas 92

6. **TOOLS FOR TEACHERS** 95
   6.1 Overview 96
   6.2 Authoring software 97

6.3 Diagnostic tools. 100
6.4 Learning management systems. 107
6.5 Interactive whiteboards 112
6.6 Focus on research 116
6.7 Classroom ideas. 118

7. TUTORIAL COURSEWARE 125
7.1 Overview. 126
7.2 Textbook-related courseware 127
7.3 Textbook-independent courseware 131
7.4 Focus on research 134
7.5 Classroom ideas. 135

8. SOCIAL SOFTWARE. 139
8.1 Overview. 140
8.2 Talking terms: Social Software vs. Web 2.0 142
8.3 Wikis. 142
8.4 Blogs and Microblogs 145
8.5 Podcasting 154
8.6 Second Life. 156
8.7 More Social Software Tools 162
8.8 Focus on research 166
8.9 Classroom ideas. 169

9. SO WHAT? 173
9.1 Value added: Developing Intercultural Agency 174
9.2 Developing Intercultural Communicative Competence (ICC) 176
9.3 Developing Autonomy 180
9.4 Developing Critical Media Literacy 183

10. TEACHING ENGLISH WITH COMPUTERS: WHAT'S NEXT? 187
10.1 Current challenges. 188
10.2 Technological Trends in Society. 190
10.3 Technology in Education 193

SUGGESTED ANSWERS FOR THE TASKS 199
BIBLIOGRAPHY 209
INDEX 217

BASIS | 1

1.1 Why a book on computers in the language classroom?

Have computers played a significant role in your own language learning biography?

Writing a book on CALL

Computers and the printed page have a complex relationship. For instance, at the outset of the computer revolution, there was the promise of the paperless office which clearly hasn't materialized (ask anybody who works in an office). Or think of 500-page manuals trying to explain to you in too small a font how to set up your new printer. So why have we decided to write a **book** on computers for the teaching and learning of languages? There are two main reasons: First of all, books are very good at structuring information and presenting it in a systematic and orderly way – at least if they are well written. Clearly, one could also think of a website where the same topic is dealt with. Unfortunately, finding reliable, well-prepared and well-structured information on the WWW can be a daunting task – or, as somebody put it, can be like trying to get a glass of water from Niagara Falls!

Secondly, we know from numerous university courses on this topic that students do appreciate a solid written document as a reliable background source for their studies. Especially in such a dynamic field as the digital world, it seems to be necessary from time to time to establish solid ground with the help of a text that outlines a complex field, offers essential explanations, and lets the reader find his or her way into the exciting field of technology-enhanced language learning.

This is exactly what we are aiming to do here – offer you a systematic, theory-driven and structured introduction to the teaching of English that is guided by digital media. We are going to describe the underlying rationale of this book later in this chapter (see 1.3) – but would like to start off with a brief historical overview of how computers have affected the language classroom in the past.

1.2 Computers in the language classroom – a brief historical overview

Do you know any milestones in computer development, and when they took place?

Personal computers – that is computers which are available to a mass public at affordable prices – have only been around for approx. 30 years (see table below). It is an understatement to say that they have changed the world, including the educational world, since. To what extent this process has really been translated into everyday classroom action is yet another matter. Nevertheless, in spite of a relatively short period of 30 years, quite a lot of research, development and publishing has taken place with regard to computers in the language classroom. Since its beginnings people have referred to this area as CALL – computer-assisted language learning. Numerous further acronyms were coined before and have been suggested since – either as attempts to replace CALL, or to identify more specific sub-areas. For example, the acronym CALL was criticized for laying too much emphasis on computers only (as opposed to other types of technology). Also the word 'assisted' seems to imply a very direct and strong influence on the language learning process. As an alternative TELL was suggested, technology-enhanced language learning, an approach drawing on various types of technology. CMC (computer-mediated communication) or NBLT (network-based language teaching) are two examples of more specific sub-areas within CALL – as their names indicate, they both focus on those online technologies which allow computer users to interact over a distance, for example through email or video chat (see chapters 2 and 3).

  For pragmatic reasons we are going to stick to the most widely established acronym – that is CALL. Clearly, CALL, defined by Levy as "the search for and study of applications of the computer in language teaching and learning" (1997: 1), is an interdisciplinary research field which gains insights from at least the following four disciplines.

A history of CALL terminology

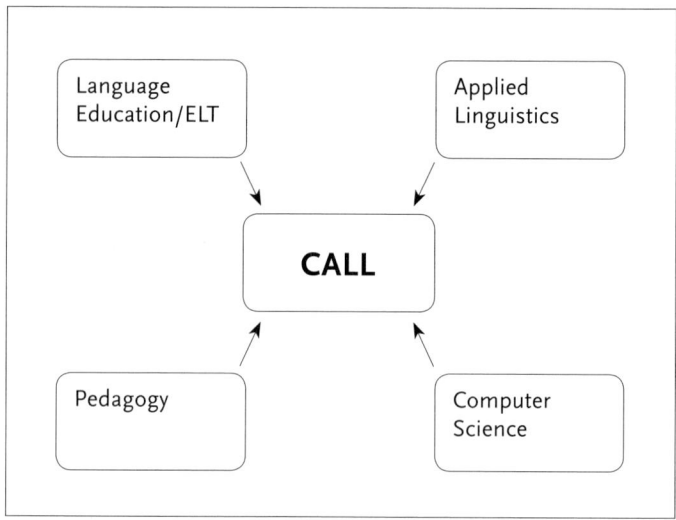

Picture 1.1: CALL and its related disciplines

CALL – an inter-
disciplinary field

The research area of language education, or English Language Teaching (ELT), plays the key role as a supporting discipline for CALL. Like most other research fields it is very heterogeneous in itself but its key interest is to focus on the language learning part in CALL (i.e. the two L's) by asking questions like: How exactly is the learning process supported by a particular computer-based activity? For example, how much sense does a gap-filling activity on missing verb forms make?

Applied linguistics has traditionally been a second major driving force in CALL, informing all kinds of applications, e.g. reference tools, or data-driven learning through corpus linguistics (chapter 4.4). Even though the term 'applied linguistics' is used differently in the international academic discourse, it usually includes the broad field of second language acquisition research (SLR) which is interested in the linguistic, psychological and social mechanisms of how human beings acquire a (first, second, third …) language. Clearly, SLR is closely connected to the above-mentioned field of ELT as well, and hence to CALL.

As a third central discipline for CALL we would suggest the broad research field of pedagogy (educational science), since whatever you do in an educational setting needs to meet sound pedagogical principles. Since CALL is such an educational setting any CALL activity also needs to be justifiable from this perspective. For instance, to what extent does a CALL scenario support the development of learner autonomy? Or does a CALL setting foster collaborative work? One could also investigate more specific research aspects from this pedagogical angle, such as the development of media literacy (2.6), or gender issues (how do boys and girls differ in the use of digital media?).

Finally, the technological dimension in CALL should be covered by its corresponding academic discipline, i.e. computer science (the 'C' in CALL). CALL only exists because there have been dramatic technological developments over the past decades, and people have sought to make use of these developments for the language learning process. Whenever there was a major new technical milestone or breakthrough (e.g. multimedia, WWW, Web 2) the question emerged as to how to exploit this also for CALL purposes. The table below gives a few examples of such software and hardware milestones.

The list of disciplines supporting CALL could even be extended beyond these four. For example, specific research and development could be done from a psychological perspective (e.g. do individual learners prefer different types of input like text, audio or video?). From the perspective of cultural studies, one could investigate intercultural learning processes in an online exchange (ch. 2.5).

For the purposes of this introductory chapter, we have now contextualized CALL within its neighbouring academic disciplines, and will next look briefly at its historical genesis.

Since its real beginnings in the sixties – well before the computer revolution of the eighties – CALL has gone through various phases which are of course clearly linked to hardware and software development on the one hand, and pedagogical and linguistic advances on the other. The following table attempts to sketch some essential trends in CALL history.

A brief historical overview

CALL – a brief historical overview							
CALL stages	Pre-history	'Behavioristic CALL'		'Communicative CALL'			Integrated CALL
CALL applications	PLATO	Vocabulary packages, grammar gap-filling	First genuine CALL software: e.g. Storyboard, simmulations	"Data-driven learning"			Webquests Learning management sytems (e,g, Moodle)
Software milestones		Micosoft founded (1975)	MS-DOS MS-Windows	WWW	e-mails Google		Youtube
Hardware milestones	Mainframe		PC IBM (1981)	Multi-media laptop			Pocket-size devices
	1940s to 1960s	1970s	1980s	Early 1990s	Late 1990s	2000-2005	Since 2006

Picture 1.2: Milestones in the development of the computer

A few explanatory notes on this overview: Clearly, up to the 1960s and well into the 1970s CALL was a largely academic endeavour, and very much restricted to computer labs at universities. Even, despite the hard- and software limitations of those days (bearing in mind that computers were the size of cupboards or bigger), some huge empirical studies relating to computer-assisted language learning (e.g. the PLATO study) were carried out. What made computers particularly interesting for all sorts of learning processes in those days was the then-prevalent learning paradigm of Behaviourism and its educational branch of 'programmed instruction'.

Behaviouristic CALL   The real CALL history seems to start with the 'microcomputer revolution' in the mid-seventies which allowed more people to experiment with the new machines and exploit them for all kinds of purposes, including the learning of languages. This development gained momentum with the availability and rapidly increasing computing power of the 'personal computer' (IBM PC, 1981) or the first Apple Macintosh (1984). Even though most software developments and applications followed a drill-and-practice pattern and still fell into the categories of "behaviouristic" CALL, first attempts were made to link CALL activities to a more communicative approach of language teaching, for example text-based simulations or games. In this context, a distinction was drawn between two different roles of the computer in the learning process – the role of the computer as a tutor vs. a tool. While the tutor function stresses the interactive dimension (immediate feedback, guided teaching in sequences), the tool function leaves more control to the learner to make use of the functions that the software offers (e.g. editing text, looking up words, searching databases). There was (and still is) some controversy about the educational value of the computer as a tutor (Trinder 2006: 150). Still, the 1990s saw a large number of new developments in both tutorial and tool directions. Two megatrends of the 1990s supported this boost – first the transformation of the formerly text-based computer into a multimedia machine that started to handle audio and images (later on video) satisfactorily, and second the fast dissemination of the WWW. While the multimedia capacities, which were largely linked to increasing computing power and CD-Rom technology, triggered a number of innovative tutorial software packages (see chapter 7), the breathtaking proliferation of the World Wide Web soon became the overwhelming driving force in CALL development. Especially the prospect of communicating via the Internet (computer-mediated communication, CMC, see above and chapters 2 and 3) introduced a new era of CALL activities which looked at the promises of the various forms of interaction between learners that the Internet can provide. There has certainly also been further progress in the tutorial sector (e.g. integration of video through DVD technology), but the overwhelming success of the Internet has marginalized many of these developments.

> Tutor vs. tool function

> The www and multimedia

> Emergence of social software

In the last ten years this trend has just seemed to continue: increasing wireless connectivity, ever smaller and faster hardware (eg smartphones, netbooks), and new 'social' web services (eg weblogs, wikis, online communities, see chapters 8 and 10) also dominate the CALL scene and its activities.

Normalization
of CALL

In a nutshell, CALL does have an eventful past despite its only being in existence 30 years. At the same time, despite all the research and the expertise gained, CALL is still far from mainstream – at least in the German school system (BMBF 2006). We have by no means reached a phase of "Integrated CALL", as Bax puts it (2003: 24), where computers are part of the everyday language classroom.

And this is where this book comes in: finding a sound place for digital media in the language classroom without giving in to any tech hype or inappropriate fears – a process that Bax simply calls 'normalisation':

> "[normalization] refers to the stage when the technology becomes invisible, embedded in everyday practice and hence 'normalised'. To take some commonplace examples, a wristwatch, a pen, shoes, writing – these are all technologies which have become normalized to the extent that we hardly recognize them as technologies" (2003: 24).

Having looked at the history of CALL, we are now going to present a way of structuring the current field of CALL.

1.3 Structuring the field of CALL – and this book

How many different computer applications do you know, and which of these might be relevant for learning languages?

Now that we have outlined the history of using computers for language learning – how can the range of computer applications and functions be categorized and put into a sensible order?

To our mind, the clearest structuring principle for CALL in general and our book in particular is based on what learners (and teachers) can do with digital media in the classroom, that is a focus on computer applications and computer-based activities. Since there is such a large number of such applications and activities, we have grouped them into five bigger content clusters and seven chapters.

Basis (Chapter 1)							
Online Communication (Chapter 2) (Chapter 3)		Materials on the Web (Chapter 4) (Chapter 5)		Tools4Teachers (Chapter 6)	Tutorial Courseware (Chapter 7)		
Written	Spoken	Web Resources	Web Research	Authoring Software, Diagnostic Tools, Learning Management Systems, Interactive Whiteboards	Textbook-Related	Textbook Independent	
		Social Software (Web 2.0) (Chapter 8)					
		Wikis, Blogs and Microblogs, Podcasting, Second Life & more social software tools					
So what? (Chapter 9)							
What's next? (Chapter 10)							

Picture 1.3: The structure of this book

Online communication currently seems to be a very dynamic area in the world of computers and we are starting off with online written and oral communication (chapters 2 and 3), followed by the second largest area, the use of the World Wide Web (chapter 4: web resources, chapter 5: web research). Then a more specific teacher perspective will be taken since a multitude of digital tools exists to support the teaching process (chapter 6). Another field of interest concerns software tools with tutorial functions (see above, historical overview), hence a single chapter will be devoted to this group of applications (see chapter 7). Afterwards we are going to focus on more recent web tools which have only emerged in the last few years and can be classified as social software (see chapter 8). Two concluding chapters will then try to summarize and evaluate all these areas, first by explicitly identifying the potential 'added value' of digital media (see chapter 9), and then by trying to anticipate future trends in CALL (see chapter 10).

Even though there are clearly overlaps between these clusters, we are convinced that this is the most transparent approach to the many possibilities that digital media have to offer for the language classroom. To further enhance transparency, each chapter sticks to a recurring structure, starting with an overview of the main theme, and finishing with a focus on research and classroom ideas. Throughout, our main concern is the learning and teaching process triggered by digital media, and not the technicalities of computer hardware and software as such.

We sincerely hope that you appreciate this approach and will find this book both informative and enjoyable!

WRITTEN ONLINE COMMUNICATION | 2

2.1 Overview

Which tools do you use to communicate via the Internet, and what are the pros and cons of each?

Clearly, communication is one of the central functions of the Internet, and the various opportunities of communicating through digital tools carry enormous potential for the language classroom. For some authors it is the main function of digital media when it comes to language learning and teaching.

Digital tools for online communication
To look at this complex field, we first make a broad distinction between written and spoken online communication, the latter being the focus of the next chapter. Furthermore, there is an overlap with social software (Web 2.0, see chapter 8) since social communities like Facebook or StudiVZ or podcasts can also contain a clear communicative element. With regard to written online communication, which is the focus of this chapter, it makes sense to further differentiate between asynchronous and synchronous writing. In a synchronous mode, like in a real conversation, the participants have to react instantly – there is no time delay between the contributions. Chatting is a perfect example of this. In an asynchronous mode, some time passes between the participants' contributions. In a non-digital world, writing a letter or a postcard is clearly asynchronous. Here, we are looking at e-mails and forums as the most prominent examples of asynchronous communication. It is evident why this distinction is vital for the classroom: synchronous or real time online communication puts the learner under a lot more time pressure, and resembles dialogic speaking. (In a chat you shouldn't spend hours looking up grammar structures if you don't want to upset your partner). E-mails, on the other hand, can usually be drafted with more care, and learners can spend more time on formal aspects, word choice etc.

The following illustration summarizes these basic distinctions and provides the basic digital tools.

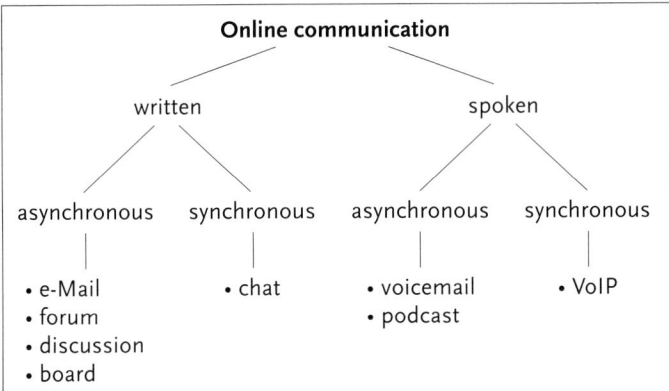

Picture 2.1: Types of online communication

2.2 Chat

Does 'chatting' feel more like 'speaking', or more like 'writing'?

The possibilities of text chat are fairly evident: it's popular among many teenage learners, it offers an authentic writing purpose, it is recordable and thus available for later reference and analysis, it is a genuine way of bringing pairs or small groups of learners together, the chat transcript is an interesting new genre, located somewhere on the writing-speaking continuum. At the same time, there are teachers (and parents) who express their reservations when it comes to chatting in the language classroom. Two arguments are repeatedly brought forward: first, how about the inevitable errors that students produce and read during the chat, and second, on a more general note, isn't chatting a fairly controversial activity in itself, with all its dangers (e.g. paedophile identity disguise) and excessive developments (e.g. cyber-bullying)? Both objections will be looked at in the light of some classroom scenarios (chapter 2.6) after clarifying some basic technical issues.

Pros and cons of chatting in the classroom

Chat tools come in different formats and layouts. They can be part of an LMS (see 6.4), and then only be accessible to a defined and limited group of learners, or they can be public with free ac-

Chat tools

cess for everybody, as is the case with countless chatrooms for all kinds of purposes. Generally, in a school context one would expect a safe chat environment with limited (and password-protected) access. This doesn't necessarily exclude commercial products like instant messaging programs (e.g. ICQ, Skype) which can be set up and run by individual users but are also "private" in the sense of access.

To further illustrate the range of possibilities that chat can offer, let's look at the following example of a grade 7 class of a German *Realschule* which conducts a regular exchange with its Norwegian partner school with English as a lingua franca

The English teachers of the two schools in Germany and Norway have decided to bring their 13- to 14-year-olds together for a regular chat exchange. Every two weeks at a set time, both classes go to the computer lab where two students on each side share one computer and chat to two students at the other end. Before the lesson, the teachers have agreed on a limited number of topics the students can choose from – of course after some introductory small talk. Topics range from current political issues (e.g. the latest political summit of world leaders) to matters of everyday life (e.g. what did you do last weekend, and what are your plans for the coming one?).

A practical example | In this example, English is used as a lingua franca, and the students are at a comparable level of competence. The main function of chat here is to trigger an authentic exchange of information between peers from different cultural backgrounds. When the chat (which may last for 30-40 minutes) is over, the chat data can later be used by the teacher. As well as focussing on the content of the students' writing, s/he can pick particular language features, e.g. repeated tense errors, stylistic issues, or spelling problems. This can be done without disclosing which student in particular might have made a mistake. This way, language work is combined with genuine communication.

While in this example English was used as a lingua franca, in a so-called 'Tandem' the students' native and target language are complementary, for example German students learning English are matched up with British students learning German. It is then agreed to use both languages to a similar extent, e.g. change over to the other language after some time has passed. Experience has shown, however, that it isn't easy to find English-speaking partners who are learning German, since for obvious reasons this combination is a lot rarer than the other way round.

In addition to the above mentioned combinations, chat exchanges can be organised in many other ways. While in our example the chats were done with a partner school on a regular basis without a particular content focus, it is probably more common to centre the chat (or e-mail) activity around one particular project that is then carried out for a certain period of time. For example, a particular novel or film is discussed, or students of different countries have to collaborate on a joint blog on their schools.

No matter what the language combination or the exact classroom setting, the added value is that is seems to be authentic. It happens in real time and therefore the difference between writing and speaking is somewhat blurred. It shares this feature – at least to some extent – with e-mails, which is an even more popular communication tool and to which we are now turning our attention.

2.3 E-Mail

Will e-mail continue to be the most popular form of communication in the Internet, or is it likely to be replaced by some other forms in the future?

While there are clear parallels between chat and e-mail projects in the language classroom, the latter has been considerably more successful: there is indeed a long tradition of using e-mails in the classroom, and to date probably thousands of e-mail exchanges between groups of learners have been carried out all over the world. In Germany this tradition is closely connected to the English teacher Reinhard Donath whose first e-mail project was recorded back in the 1980s and who still runs a highly recommended website on this topic (www.englisch.schule.de/email). One reason for its popularity is certainly the fact that e-mails are still a firmly established part of our everyday lives. There are countless e-mail providers with free services, e-mails are the

The tradition of e-mail projects

most convenient way of sending attachments like documents or pictures, and e-mails are no longer restricted to computers but can be sent to the various mobile devices. In schools teachers as well as learners as well are increasingly making use of e-mails to deliver assignments and other learning materials – even though it is of course the teacher's responsibility to make sure that all his or her learners do have access. Besides this out of class use, e-mails especially come into play in so-called key pal exchanges. Just like pen friends (or pen pals) write letters to each other regularly, in e-mail projects learners are matched up to exchange e-mails. Such projects can take many shapes, as covered in the chapter on chats before, some essential questions are:

Parameters for e-mail projects

- which language is used (English as lingua franca, or Tandem?)
- what is the time frame (regular exchange, including out-of-class content, or limited project duration?)
- do students work individually at each end, or in pairs (or even groups of three or four?)

Common models for online intercultural exchanges

Beyond such basic considerations it is of course crucial to have clear objectives about the exchange, be it concerning aspects of language practice, the intercultural encounter with a particular target culture, the preparation of a real class trip later that year, or the general development of media literacy (e.g. forms of politeness).

| e-Tandem | The original idea for this concept was developed at the university of Bochum (see slf.ruhr-uni-bochum.de/etandem for more information). E-Tandems are teams of learners who communicate through any channel available through the net, e.g. e-mail, chat or Skype. It is a bilateral concept, i.e. the partners learn from each other which necessitates that both partners want to learn each other's native language. In e-tandem projects in school classes a common arrangement is that half of the message is written in the target language and half of the message in one's native language. In many cases part of the deal is that errors in the target language texts are corrected by the respective native speaker and feedback is given. For more information on e-Tandems also see O'Rourke 2007. |
| Cultura | Projects that are organized along the lines of the cultura concept focus, as the name suggests, on cultural aspects. The idea was first developed at the Massachusetts Institute of Technology in the 1990ies for a cultural exchange with France but has been adapted by various researchers (see García & Caprota 2007). Cultural or seemingly global issues, such as living with one's parents (Garcia & Caprota 2007) or cultural issues that are |

	raised in a film or book, are first discussed in class and then with the partner group. Often a cultura project will start with a questionnaire, the discussion of the results of the respective groups in class and then in exchanges and forums online. Both groups write in their mother tongues as the belief is that only then will they be able to convey their ideas effectively. This again implies that both groups are learning the respective other group's language. The difference to the other concepts described above is that students will only read texts in the target language, they will not produce the language within the project. While originally e-mails or forums were used in cultura projects, newer projects are now also carried out with the help of wikis (see www3.unileon.es/personal/wwdfmrod/ for more information).
e-Twinning	eTwinning is the name of an EU project that connects school in the long term. eTwinning differs from the other two concepts, in that it does not prescribe any kind of structure, content or form of language use. There are technological and pedagogical principles governing the initiative however, e.g. the use of ICT and the development of a European identity in the schools involved, the idea of innovation taking place through teachers interacting and exchanging ideas, the goal of establishing a European network of schools and the aim of supporting students' intercultural awareness (see Domíngues Miguela 2007). The schools that are part of the eTwinning network interact in a secured environment on joint projects. English is often used as a lingua franca as the links are made between any of the European countries, i.e. in most cases there are no native speakers of English involved. See etwinning.de for more information.

Table 2.1: Common types of intercultural exchanges

Notwithstanding these and other decisions, it makes sense to consider e-mail projects from the process-oriented view of task-based language teaching and sub-divide them into a pre, while and post stage. Well before the beginning of an exchange, teachers must get into contact to negotiate the exchange details (e.g. tools, topics, time frame), but also learners need to be prepared (e.g. purpose of the exchange, necessary technical skills, preparation of materials). During the exchange, the teacher mainly turns into a troubleshooter, solving technical problems, helping with the writing process, reminding students to be reliable exchange partners etc. From the learners' perspective this main stage of an e-mail project is structured by the different tasks they are supposed to accomplish. Even though generalisations are difficult here and a lot depends on the learners' age, experience and the

Stages of e-mail projects

purposes of the exchange, here are some typical tasks in an e-mail exchange (inspired by R. Donath, see website above):

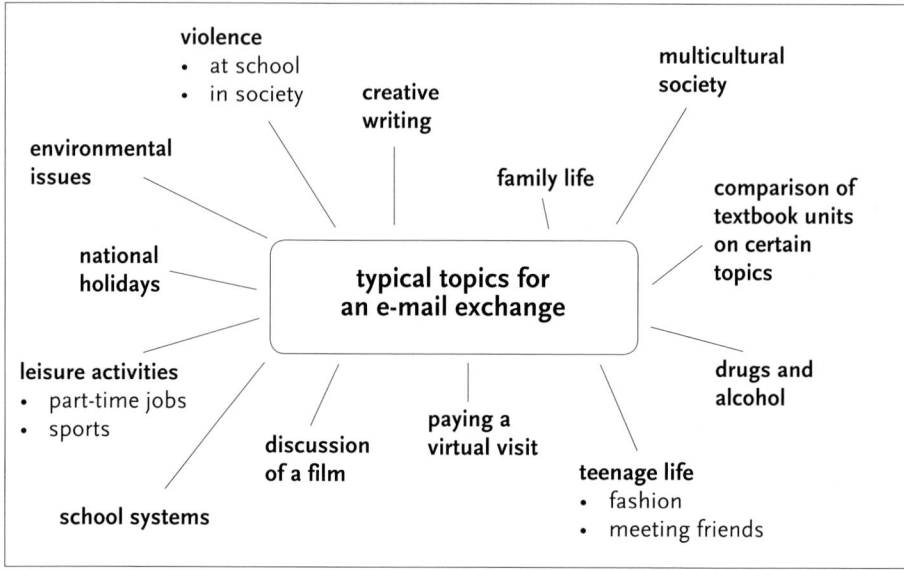

Picture 2.2: Typical topics for an e-mail exchange

If time permits, teachers can already build in phases of discussion and assessment while the exchange is (still) running, drawing learners' attention to language aspects as well as discussing positions that were expressed in the e-mails. Here it is a good idea for teachers to browse through their learners' e-mails and simply copy and paste elements that may be relevant for classroom use.

This assessment can (and should be) more systematic after the exchange is over. Besides plenary discussions on content or language it should be inherent in every such project that learners spend some time on an honest evaluation: What did I learn from the project? What did I like best/least? What should be done differently next time?

Potential pitfalls during e-mail projects

Having outlined these basics, maybe a word of caution regarding e-mail projects is required. First of all, it should not be forgotten that even though e-mails are a well-established tool, managing an exchange with 30 learners can be quite challenging for all kinds of technical reasons. You as a teacher should have access to the learners' e-mails, passwords, etc. Technically, it might therefore be easier to use a forum or discussion board instead (see 4.4). Secondly, a lot depends on the reliability of your partner (and yourself, of course!). It is very frustrating, particularly for younger learners if their partner(s) fail to respond, or one side takes the exchange less seriously than the other. A working and reliable partnership, often with one of the partner schools is therefore precious and needs to be looked after.

Thirdly, we need to stress the open nature of such projects and their less predictable outcome. Unlike a textbook activity with its predicted results, e-mail exchanges depend to a large extent on the individual's willingness and ability to engage, and to be open-minded and curious. As a teacher you play a vital role in sorting out technical and administrative issues, creating the right atmosphere and setting appropriate tasks but authentic communication between people can't be predicted (e.g. remain superficial or end in conflict). We are addressing this issue in our research focus of this chapter (2.5).

Despite these warnings let us assure you from our many positive experiences that such cultural encounters (often) lead to positive learning processes. It is therefore worth taking the risk. Forums, or discussion boards are a similar tool for achieving this.

2.4 Forums, discussion boards, bulletin boards

Where in the Internet do you encounter this form of communication, and what are their specific strengths?

The chapter on forums, also known as discussion or bulletin boards, will be considerably shorter than the last since much of what was said about e-mail projects also applies to this mode of online communication. As can be seen in the forum screenshot, from a didactic perspective the biggest difference between forums and e-mails is that forums allow every user to read everybody else's text easily – in other words they are rather like public e-mailing. Another distinctive feature from an educational angle is the spe-

Characteristic features of forums

cific structure discussion boards offer through their system of threads. Threads give the ongoing discussion a clear format because you can immediately see which message introduces a new topic or is a reply, and who is referring to which topic.

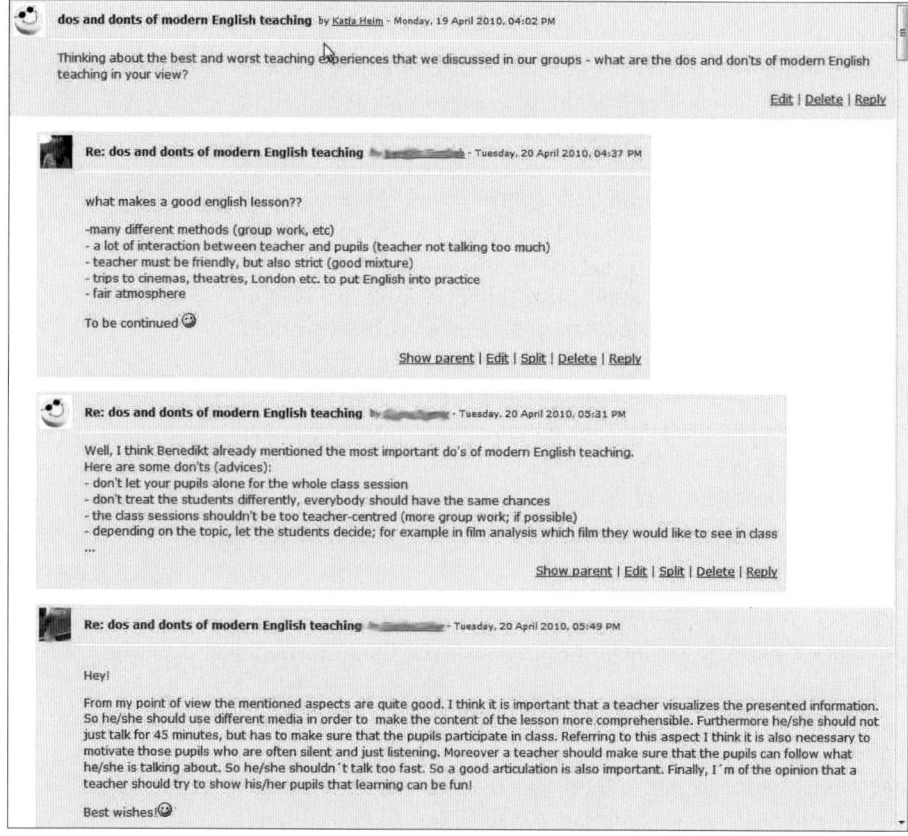

Screenshot 2.1: A forum discussion within Moodle

Integration of forums into sites and tools

In teaching and learning contexts forums are typically embedded in a learning management system (as in the screenshot above, see ch. 6.4 as well), but they can also be installed as a single tool (the platform 'Lehrer Online', for instance, offers a stand-alone forum tool, see www.lo-net2.de). Increasingly, though, the basic idea of 'leaving a message' for others or discussing certain matters publicly can be found all over the Internet – just think of online magazines or bookshops where people can leave their comments on articles and books or reply to other people's statements. In a way blogs can also serve a similar function (see ch. 8.4), and finally there are also tools which allow you to leave audio rather than text comments (eg the 'Wimba Voice Board, see ch. 3.2).

Even though most teachers seem to be a lot more familiar with e-mails we are convinced that in a typical keypal exchange forums are often the more appropriate tool, exactly for the two pedagogic reasons mentioned above – the simultaneous availability of all the comments, and their straightforward thread structure. As to the first argument we found that more advanced and older learners especially seem to appreciate this access to their classmates' writing and also profit from it linguistically. So far this observation is largely anecdotal, and we are not aware of any published empirical evidence which backs up this impression. Nevertheless, quite a lot of research has gone into the whole field of computer-mediated communication, and we are taking a brief look at this research in the next section.

Forums in online exchanges

2.5 Focus on Research

What are some controversial issues with regard to written online communication, and how could they be turned into a research question?

Written online communication, as outlined in this chapter, has been in existence for more than 20 years. Consequently, it has also given rise to quite a few research activities. As way of example, Belz has investigated the social and individual backgrounds of students and the influence this has on the success of online exchanges (2001), O'Rourke has explored how tandem exchanges (see 2.3) can contribute to the development of learner autonomy (2007), or Müller-Hartmann has addressed the question of task efficiency, i.e. how tasks are to be set up and which qualities they should possess to stimulate efficient learning outcomes (2000). Furthermore, various authors have provided an overview of the research that has been done in this field of computer-

Failure in online exchanges

mediated communication (e.g. Kern & Warschauer 2000, O'Dowd 2007), and the online journal 'Language Learning & Technology' lists more than fifty research papers under the CMC heading (go to llt.msu.edu, previous issues). While many of these investigations seem to confirm the learning potential of online communication, success can by no means be guaranteed, and whether or not the various CMC scenarios achieve their desired outcome depends on various factors. O'Dowd & Ritter (2006) have tried to offer a systematic overview of factors which have repeatedly led to 'failure' in telecollaborative exchanges. The illustration below summarizes their findings by identifying ten such factors which can lead to a breakdown in communication or prevent learners from taking full advantage of an exchange. These factors can be classified as belonging to four different levels – an individual, a classroom, a socio-institutional, and an interaction level.

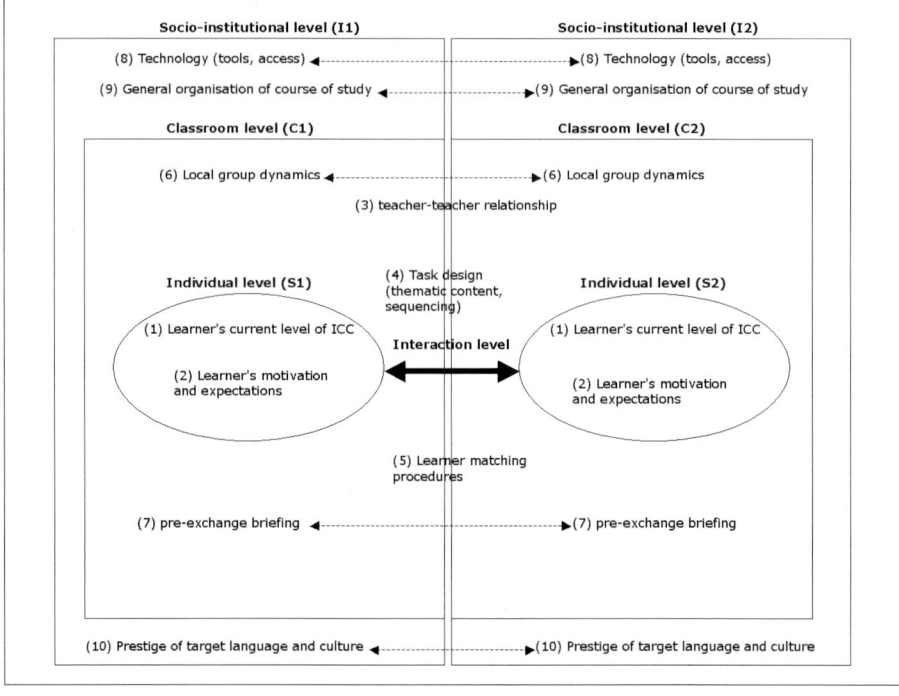

Table 2.3: Reasons for failed communication in telecollaborative exchanges

The individual level describes the personal and the educational background of the learner. Of special interest regarding failed communication are the single learner's intercultural communicative competence as well as his expectations and motivation. The classroom level is subdivided into teacher-teacher relationships, task design and thematic content, learner matching procedures, local group dynamics and pre exchange briefing between the tutors of the exchange. In order to prevent problems or a communication breakdown at the classroom level, a rigorous process of advance planning and consultation between students and teachers may be useful. Compared to the classroom level, the socioinstitutional level goes beyond the actual classroom interaction. On this level possible reasons for failed communication are technology, differences in prestige values of cultures and languages, or general organisational aspects of the participants' context, for example, misalignment of academic calendars. Finally, the interaction between learners can itself lead to misunderstandings and tension which may arise from cultural differences in communicative style and behaviour.

Notwithstanding such challenges, research should continue to investigate the huge learning potential of online communication. One research issue that still seems to be fairly open and has attracted recent research is the important question as to what extent written online communication can lead to a more systematic development of grammatical competence and correctness in the learners' developing L2. O'Dowd & Ware, for instance have investigated how online exchange projects can help students to notice and further develop language forms. They suggest specific 'focus on form' stages within an exchange which allow learners to reflect upon their own patterns of error and to trace their individual language development (2008). However, they emphasize the vital role of the teacher in guiding students through such stages and offering expert support.

In summary, research in the field of written online communication is already fairly advanced and has shed some light on the prerequisites and conditions of successful online learning. Such investigations should by all means be continued at all levels of research – from small-scale teacher initiated classroom-based action research to larger quantitative studies that try to prove the efficiency of CMC empirically.

2.6 Classroom Ideas

Have you ever been involved in written online communication for language learning purposes – at school, university, or at your own initiative? If yes, how successful was it?

A possible 'classroom idea' has already been briefly outlined in the passage on chatting in this chapter (2.2). This can of course be adapted to other writing tools like e-mail or bulletin boards. Here, rather than offering another example, we would like to provide a checklist of ten crucial aspects that need to be considered when preparing for a keypal project.

– **Main aim**: what is the main purpose of the exchange (eg language practice, preparing a class trip, intercultural aspects)?
– **Language**: English as a lingua franca, or Tandem principle?
– **Partner**: what do you know about the partner?
– **Grouping**: how are learners grouped together (individually, pairs, groups, even distribution, or different group size on each side)?
– **Tasks**: which activities, topics, tasks are planned? How do they relate to the syllabus or the coursebook?
– **Time frame**: how long is the exchange going to last? How often do learners exchange information or meet online?
– **Tools**: which software tools are used at which stage of the project (chat, e-mail, forum, LMS ...)?
– **Recording**: is learner input stored and available for later analysis?
– **Assessment**: are learners given grades in the course of the exchange (eg in a project folder)?
– **Error treatment**: what is the project policy on dealing with incorrect or inappropriate language?

Much of what has been said in this chapter on written online communication also holds true for spoken online communication projects which will be the focus of the next chapter. Indeed, more complex classroom projects often go for a combination of both modes.

Tasks

1. Reflect on your own practices of written online communication. Which tools do you use? How often do you use them? Under which circumstances/with whom? Which do you like best/least?

2. In the context of media literacy and Internet safety, familiarize yourself with the British portal 'Childnet International' (www. childnet-int.org), and the various Childnet projects.

3. Check under www.englisch.schule.de/email.htm what advice Reinhard Donath offers with regard to e-mail projects.

4. Find a forum where people discuss learning and teaching related issues (eg in groups.yahoo.com). Ideally, join a forum, leave a (meaningful!) message and see what happens.

5. Go to the online journal 'Language Learning & Technology' (http://llt.msu.edu). Open the archive and browse – via topic – one article listed under "computer-mediated communication".

6. Go to the ‚Online TESL Journal‚ (http://iteslj.org). Find out what TESL stands for and search the website for information on e-mail projects in the language classroom.

ORAL ONLINE COMMUNICATION | 3

3.1 Overview

How will the ratio between written and oral communication on the Internet develop in the next couple of years? Will writing still be dominant?

As illustrated in the overview of chapter 2, it makes sense to draw a distinction between oral and written online communication (see 2.1). Even though there is a large overlap between the two and many communication tools allow for both written and oral modes of communication (e.g. Skype, see below), the ever-increasing importance of spoken online communication demands a chapter of its own in the context of CALL. It will be considerably shorter than chapter 4, though, since some basic distinctions can be made here – for instance the division between synchronous (3.2) vs. asynchronous oral communication (3.3). The subsequent subchapters will then follow the pattern of the other chapters in the book, i.e. a glimpse at research (3.4), followed by some ideas for the classroom (3.5).

3.2 Synchronous oral communication

In what way is spoken communication through the Internet different from using a telephone?

Development of synchronous oral communication — Audio and video conferencing are the two main key words when it comes to spoken communication in real time. Undoubtedly, this field is currently one of the fastest growing in the online digital world and closely connected to mass broadband and flat-rate availability in many countries. Technically, both audio and video conferencing have been around for quite some time, and experiments with audio conferencing in language learning date back more than ten years (Hampel & Hauck 2004). The term "conferencing" implies the notion that contrary to telephoning, more than two partners can easily be connected in a "conference". At the time of writing, some leading tools in its field are Skype, ICQ, Windows Live Manager, Adobe Connect or iChat for

Apple computers. When used for video conferencing, these tools rely on a multimedia PC with a microphone, loudspeakers and a webcam. In contrast to such desktop videoconferencing, there are also technical devices on a larger scale where groups of people sit in front of a large screen and can see their partners as a group (room-based video conferencing).

It goes without saying that the free availability of such software opens up enormous new possibilities for the classroom. It connects the language learner with other speakers- native or non-native-in a way that comes closes to face to face communication. In contrast to written modes of transmission there is even less time to plan what you want to say and to react to what your partner says. In a conference mode, where the speakers take turns it can become quite challenging, especially when there is no video support to visualize your interlocutor(s). Additionally, all this takes place in a digital environment with further tools: programs like Skype or ICQ offer text chat alongside the audio/ video connection, or users can transmit their computer screen, file attachment etc. to their partners. It is quite accepted, then, that spoken online communication between learners from different cultural backgrounds who usually do not know each other before the exchange is both an exciting and demanding undertaking. A lot of care has to go into the planning and organization of such learning scenarios, and only a small number of results have been gathered in the last years. Some initial findings and ideas will be presented below (3.4 and 3.5). Before that, let's turn our attention to less obvious fields of asynchronous spoken communication.

Synchronous oral communication in the classroom

3.3 Asynchronous oral communication

What kind of communication is your message on a friend's answering machine?

As a postscript to the previous chapter and an introduction to the possibilities of asynchronous spoken communication, we would like to remind you that real time communication can easily be recorded.

Tools for creating audio files

Various freely available tools directly record the ongoing audio transmission and turn it into an mp3-file. Just like chat data (see 3.2) teachers can later analyze such recordings and look for language-related issues (e.g. use of particular structures, word choice, errors) or content matter (e.g. degree of politeness or directness, range of topics). Students and teachers alike can return to their recordings and examine them for specific characteristics. In this respect, communication becomes "asynchronous" since it is accessible for later use. But there are further reasons for audio and video recordings, and hence asynchronous oral communication. Audio editors like Audacity or NanoGong enable users to record their voices, edit the recordings, integrate them into websites, or just send them somewhere as a file. Similarly, there are video editors (e.g. Windows Movie Maker, TokBox, iMovie) for video production and video messaging. It is of course debatable whether this is still "communication". Is somebody "communicating" when uploading a video to youtube? While we do not want to engage in this academic debate here, we certainly want to stress the language learning possibilities such audio and video messaging offers.

Podcasts in the EFL classroom

Technically, the most significant application in this context is podcasting which is at the same time one of the most prominent developments in the Web 2 context (see chapter 8). There is probably no need for a definition of the term or a description of its technical background (see Wikipedia entry, if you are interested), but a brief word on its use for language learning purposes seems imperative. Clearly the most obvious use is the distribution of (authentic) listening material, which can also be downloaded by mobile devices like MP3-players. Countless websites like the BBC, commercial distributors like iTunes (also for Windows PCs), or educational portals like 'lehrer-online.de' offer authentic podcasts for a free download and lots of advice on integrating podcasts into the language classroom.

A second strand is the production and publication of the learners' own podcasts – either for their classmates or an even broader audience. All that is needed is an audio editor (e.g. Audacity, see above) and server space to upload the podcasts (either your local school server or an external host like 'podhost.de' or 'mypodcast.com').

Even though podcasting still is a relatively new technological development a number of teachers have begun to explore its potential for the classroom (see the section on podcasting on www.englisch.schule.de, or schulpodcasting.info for examples, and chapters 3.4 and 3.5 for research and classroom ideas).

Apart from listening to or producing podcasts, there are further audio and video tools which allow for more specific forms of asynchronous oral communication. With programs like Wimba or Voxopop, for instance, one can create 'oral' discussion boards that function more or less like their written equivalents (see chapter 2.4), i.e. learners record their messages in response to other statements or indeed any task, and all the recordings are displayed like a threaded discussion. With a tool like Tokbox, this idea can even be extended to video messaging.

'Oral' discussion boards

The question remains, of course, as to how such tools can be integrated into classroom work, and when these oral tools are superior to their written counterparts. One would imagine that many students prefer the directness and ease of spoken communication – synchronous or asynchronous – and this is probably often the case. However, O'Dowd quotes from an end-of-exchange feedback where learners (American and Spanish University students) were asked to compare the two:

> "I prefer the written one because it's easier to write than speaking. It would be easier to speak if we could see them but talking to a computer screen is not very personal.
>
> It's easier to understand them in the written forum because on the spoken forum we have to listen to the recordings at least twice to catch the idea" (2007: 12).

This example shows that a lot of factors come into play when using audio or video for online communication. The subsequent overview of research activities in this field will serve to underline this impression.

3.4 Focus on Research

How does it 'feel' to communicate orally via the Internet with some-
body you haven't met before? What challenges are there, and how
can they be dealt with?

Research on
Asynchronous oral
communication

As said above, spoken online communication through the Internet – both synchronous and asynchronous – is a more recent
development because it requires more computing power and
bandwidth which have only been widely available for the last few
years. Consequently, less research has been conducted in this
field than in the field of written online communication. However,
there are a number of studies investigating various aspects connected with spoken language in virtual communication. For instance, Volle (2005) and Ducate & Lomicka (2009) present studies focussing on the acquisition and development of speaking
skills through the Ducate & Lomicka (2009) use of audio e-mails
and podcasting. Even though their findings are mixed and one
cannot assume that a few online sessions will automatically lead
to better pronunciation or intonation (see studies for more details), both papers highlight the potential of (asynchronous)
speaking. Hampel & Hauck (2004) have looked into real-time
(i.e. synchronous) audio-conferencing which was embedded in a
distance education setting at the Open University in Britain. According to these researchers, a lot of care has to go into the development of a pedagogical framework and the development of
appropriate tasks to turn audio-conferencing into a successful
learning experience. Indeed, task design is considered a crucial
aspect of any kind of computer-mediated communication.
O'Dowd & Ware (2009) offer a survey of existing studies and
classify them according to the tasks that were developed and
carried out. Even though this overview is based on written rather
than spoken online communication, it provides a useful outline
of task types and their underlying intentions. The following table
is a synopsis of their findings (a more detailed table is available
in the original article).

Task	Description	Aims
- Information exchange tasks -		
Authoring 'Cultural Autobio-graphies"	Students present themselves and their home cultures to partners through cultural autobiographies in visual and textual formats	Establishing personal relationship/ increasing awareness for cultural differences
Carrying out virtual Interviews	Students alternate with interviewing each other on cultural themes and produce a class presentation/written report on interview process	Development of intercultural communicative competence (ICC)
Engaging in informal discussions	Students are given general questions (e.g. 'How do the new technologies influence your life?') or a cultural product from their culture or the target culture (e.g. newspaper article/ film)	Learner independence/ development of fluencyin target language
Exchanging story Collections	Each class alternately collects legends, folk tales or accounts of local historical events from their partner class. A class magazine or website can then be published with the resulting collection.	Increased factual/cultural knowledge about target culture
-Comparison and Analysis-		
Comparing parallel texts	Both classes study, compare and analyse pieces of literature/ films/fairy tales from both cultures which are based on a common theme	Increased awareness of target culture and one's own culture
Comparing class question-naires	Both classes complete questionnaires (e.g. related to word associations, reactions to situations) and compare answers. Discussion of findings is done online	Developing an awareness of different cultural meanings/ connotations of words/concepts in both cultures
Analysing cultural Products	Cultural products from both cultures (films, pieces of literature, items in tourist shops) are analysed and discussed by both groups	Greater awareness of target culture/one's own culture
Translating	Students translate text from their language to target language. Without seeing original, students from target culture help to refine and correct the translation	Improved language awareness/development of linguistic accuracy and fluency in target language

-Collaboration and product creation-		
Collaborating on product creation	Students in both classes work together to produce a document (e.g. essay) or multi-media product (e.g. website/powerpoint presentation)	Development of intercultural communicative competence (ICC)/ electronic literacy
Transforming text Genres	Students in culture 1 help culture 2 partners to rewrite texts in a different genre in their target language	Improved metalinguistic awareness/linguistic accuracy + fluency in target language
Carrying out 'closed outcome' discussions	Students from both cultures share and compare information while completing an information gap activity (e.g. a 'spot the difference' activity based on different versions of pictures)	Negotiation of meaning/ development of linguistic accuracy and fluency in target language
Making cultural translations/ adaptations	Students from both cultures make a culturally appropriate translation/adaptation of a product from either culture (e.g. film scene/ TV commercials)	Development of intercultural communicative competence (ICC)

Table 3.1: Overview of telecollaborative tasks (O'Dowd & Ware 2009)

It is difficult to anticipate how spoken online communication will develop over the next years and to what extent it is going to replace writing (see introductory question of chapter 3). We expect that its importance will increase dramatically with more powerful and flexible digital tools. This trend should be taken up for language learning purposes, especially since oral proficiency is a key skill in the language classroom and has often been neglected in the past. This trend would also imply a call for more research in this field. For example, an interesting research question would be to investigate the different language constellations. What difference does it make to communicate orally with somebody whose native language is English and who learns German (i.e. Tandem principle), vs. communication with English as a lingua franca (see also 2.2)?

3.5 Classroom ideas

How can written and spoken online communication be combined in the classroom? Which digital tools could be brought together for such a purpose?

Naturally, classroom projects focusing on oral online communication can be set up according to similar principles as in the case of projects with a focus on writing (see checklist in 2.6). Indeed, often a combination of speaking and writing tools (e.g. Skype) is the ideal choice when learners use both modes to communicate.

At Pennsylvania State University, researchers have set up a 'computer mediated activity library' with 50 project examples. The following table presents a selection of ten chat and audio voice activities aiming at different language skills and topics.

Activity	Topic	Aims	Description of activity
Admission Board (Writing project via chat)	Culture/ Competing for admission to a renowned university	Language as a means of persuasion/ focus on polite expressions and cultural	Students are either a candidate or a member of the admission board and play their respective part in the chat room. Candidates can prepare a statement before engaging in the discussion. Eventually the board selects one future student
Doctor, doctor (Spoken communication: podcasts)	Miscellaneous health-related aspects	Focus is on appropriateness (e.g. vocabulary), length, accuracy, fluency etc.	Patients leave a voice mail for their doctor asking for advice. Doctors reply by leaving them a message
Good deal gone bad (Written communication via chat)	Business/ Complaint management	Interactional and pragmatic competence	Buyer and seller chat about a broken DVD player. The client demands refunding, while the seller is upset that the invoice remains uncleared

On the news (Spoken communi- cation: podcasts)	News from English- speaking countries and culture	pragmatic competence	Groups produce a clearly structured podcast on any current topic on the news including e.g. an interview with an expert
Language and society (Written communi- cation: chat)	Linguistic diversity (of English and in English- speaking countries)	conversational moves/ discourse strategies/ dealing with multiple perspectives on a controversial topic	Students familiarize themselves with English dialects and a) discuss e.g. the position of a standard, how this is taught, what role minority languages/ dialects play etc. b) engage in a discussion concern- ing a possible cut of funding for education in regional dialects/ languages
The mayor is dead (Written communi- cation: chat)	Role play with the aim of finding out who murdered the mayor	conversational discourse strate- gies/ question formation/ critical deduction skills/ interpretation of written and spoken language	Group of approx. 10 students is assigned roles that they play in a chat room, while being interrogated by a detective

Table 3.2: Sample projects for online spoken communication (taken from calper.la.psu.edu/ cmc/index.php)

Preventing cyberbullying

As another classroom idea we would like to draw your attention to the British website digizen.org which offers a multitude of resources to strengthen learners' media literacy and develop their awareness and understanding of what can be called 'digital citi- zenship'. This focus goes somewhat beyond a genuine online exchange project but of course the use of communication tools goes hand in hand with this focus on electronic literacy. Ques- tions like internet safety, privacy issues, or cyberbullying can be addressed alongside such a project. Among many other materi- als, digizen.org offers the award-winning short film 'Let's fight it together' which deals with the highly urgent issue of cyberbullying in a very effective way.

Tasks

1. Go to Nik Peachley's 'Learning Technology Blog' where you can find lots of examples on spoken online communication projects, and have a closer look at one of his suggestions or resources (http://nikpeachey.blogspot.com/).

2. If you are not familiar with audio-conferencing software as mentioned in this chapter (e.g. Skype, Windows Live Manager, Adobe Connect or iChat for Apple computers), try one out, and see how long it takes to get used to it (e.g. turn-taking with more than two participants, using text chat alongside speaking). Also, try to record one of your sessions and listen to it.

3. Go to www.schulpodcasting.info and familiarize yourself with the many suggestions that are made for using podcasts in the language classroom.

4. Watch the short film 'Let's fight it together' on cyberbullying (www.digizen.org) and think of a lesson scenario for the film.

5. Go to the 'Computer mediated Activity Library' mentioned in 3.5 (see table 3.2 for web address), and choose one of the 50 suggested activities for closer investigation. How could your activity be modified to fit a teaching context you are familiar with?

WEB RESOURCES | 4

4.1 Overview

What kinds of resources do you normally look out for on the web?

In most classrooms textbooks are still the main resource (Müller-Hartmann & Schocker-von Ditfurth 2011). While we are far from suggesting – especially to beginner teachers – not working with a textbook at least as guidance, we certainly believe that the World Wide Web has an increasing number of alternative or additional materials to offer. Over the last few years the web has become a most comprehensive resource for basically everyone and for all different kinds of purposes, i.e. also for learners and teachers of English – the offering sites ranging from those with useful links to fully blown learning environments and material collections. The vast amount and the diversity of resources make it quite difficult and time-consuming to find appropriate materials and to judge which are of high quality and which are not.

In this chapter we set out to provide an overview of the most common and the most useful sites for learners and teachers, i.e. while we do assume that you are familiar with how to use of the internet, we also assume that you are not fully aware of all the useful sites and facets of the web for you as a teacher. We won't be able to provide you with a complete overview – our approach is rather to give concrete examples of some useful web portals and reference tools.

4.2 Web and internet: a brief definition of terms

Web and internet: Where do you see the difference?

Web vs. Internet   The terms internet and World Wide Web are often used interchangeably. In the technical sense they are not synonyms however. The word internet refers to the infrastructure of the network, i.e. the manner in which millions of computers all over the world are technically linked. The internet is decentralized – each internet computer, called host, can be seen as an individual centre in itself that is linked with all the other centres in the world.

The word World Wide Web (www), or short web, refers to the web of contents that is created with the help of the internet. The web makes use of the infrastructure of the internet. The documents on the www are linked and can be viewed because they all use codes that are readable by a web browser such as the Internet Explorer or Firefox.

4.3 Web Portals

What is a web portal and what can you find there?

In the architectural sense a portal is a huge and imposing entrance into something. Likewise web portals serve as an entry, either into a number of pages on a particular topic or for a bundle of applications that are used frequently. In both cases the web portal provides us with an overview and structure that makes it easy for us to find the applications or the information we are interested in. The number and the importance of portals are growing as they help making the diverse offers on the web more accessible for users. Some portals seem to be growing into all comprising sites which offer all the applications that users might need on the web. While some of the applications lend themselves to searching the web (see chapter 3), others contain interesting contents for groups of people such as EFL teachers and learners who can make use of portals in many different ways.

> Web portal: a definition

If the aim of our language lessons is to enable students to take part in everyday life using the target language, our lessons and also the materials we choose should mirror this aim. The use of authentic materials provides us with the opportunity of discussing issues that are of importance outside the classroom and potentially also for students. This makes it more likely that students will be interested in engaging with the contents of the materials, provided the issues are chosen well and are used in a task-based learning environment (see Willis & Willis 2007; Müller-Hartmann & Schocker-von Ditfurth 2004), that allows the learners to interact with the materials and others in a meaningful way.

> Using Authentic materials

Portals of TV Channels and Newspapers

TV channels as well as the major newspapers have web portals and offer up to date news on the web as well as in the conventional way. More and more people only read the news online which has already led to some publishers considering abandoning the printed version. All major newspapers, magazines and TV channels have an elaborate online section and, are interesting resources for analysing different types of styles of communication.

The BBC web portal A portal which has huge potential for use in language lessons is the website belonging to the British TV channel the BBC, with written, audio and video-news plus an abundance of additional materials. As British English and culture still plays a major role in English lessons, this portal offers an almost inexhaustible source of materials for teachers. The BBC portal combines many different services. From the main site one can access completely different sections, such as top stories of the day in written form as well as audio or video files. Also, there are big sections on business, sport, the world service, travel, TV channels, radio and weather among others. Each chosen sub-category links with new services, some of which can be regarded as sub-portals in themselves. The link to the "Learning English" part of the site, for example, is a huge portal for learners and teachers of English, the BBC children's site is a portal into different applications and sites

Web portals of newspapers and TV channels that are of interest to children. The BBC Learning English site and the children's site both provide simplified versions of current news as well as other materials that can also be understood by younger and less advanced learners.

Name	Description
Times Online timesonline.co.uk	The online version of one of the most traditional British quality papers. Some parts, such as the jobs section or the educational supplement, can only be viewed by registered, i.e. paying users.
The Guardian guardian.co.uk	An online version of another very traditional quality paper in the UK which has always been slightly more left wing than the Times; with many different sub sections. All sections can be viewed for free.

The Sun thesun.co.uk	The online version of the most well-known tabloid paper in the UK with the same style of news and layout as the printed version.
The Daily Mirror mirror.co.uk	Another online version of a UK yellow tabloid paper.
The BBC portal bbc.co.uk	A big portal with up to date information in written, audio and video versions and links to interest or target group related sub-portals
The BBC site for children bbc.co.uk/children	This is a news portal for children with easy-to-understand articles, videos and audio files as well as games. Although the texts might still be too complex for absolute beginners, this is a very valuable site that can be used as a resource by learners and teachers.
Sky News news.sky.com/ skynews	Online portal belonging to the British private news channel with written articles and up to date videos on the latest issues.
The Australian theaustralian. news.com.au	The online version of the most widely sold Australian national quality newspaper. There are links to articles on current affairs in Australia as well as abroad. Also, there are job adverts, links to a real estate site for browsing properties for sale and also a very useful section with links to other online versions, e.g. to new.scom.au.
CNN cnn.com	The online portal for the internationally famous US news channel CNN (Cable News Network). The majority of news on line are articles written on current issues. There is a video section, however, with a selection of video clips on international news.
The New York Times nytimes.com	Big online portal for the renowned American quality newspaper which still has the biggest editorial staff in the US. The emphasis is put more and more on the online platform which also integrates video and audio.
Mail & Guardian mg.co.za	The online version of South Africa's biggest and most popular quality newspaper, including the famous Zapiro and Madam & Eve cartoons.
Al Jazeera english.**aljazeera.**net	English version of the Arabic-language news network. It can be a good source for alternative viewpoints on current international affairs with articles and videos about news in different regions in the world as well as on different topics, such as business or sport.

Table 4.1: A collection of important newspapers & news channels in the English speaking world

Portals with Video- and Audio Clips

The above mentioned news sites do include audio- and video-clips on current issues and selected topics of interest. There are whole databases with film- and audio clips, however. A big number of sites have evolved, with, at the time of writing, youtube. com being the most famous of all.

Searching the
YouTube site

It is common knowledge that whether one is looking for a short, funny Mr. Bean clip, the prologues in different Romeo and Juliet film productions, a music video, speeches by politicians, clips from sitcoms, BBC nature and science programmes, talk shows or amateur theatre productions by other school classes, it can all be found on YouTube. Viewing the contents on the site is legal, so there should not be any problem using the resources, unless the site has been blocked by the web administrators at your school in general.

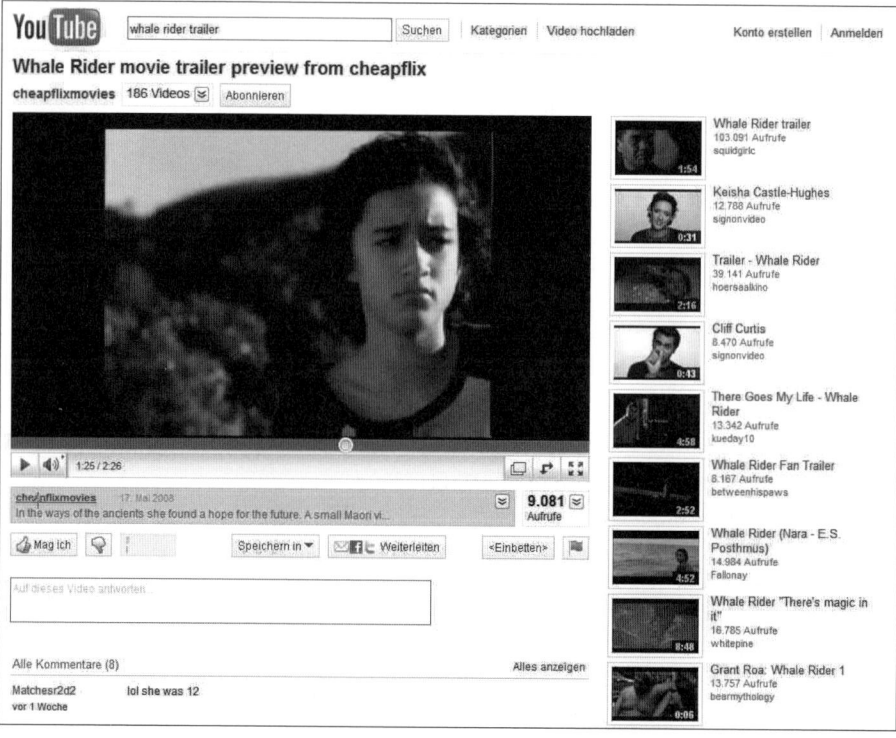

Screenshot 4.1: A Film Clip from *The Whale Rider* on YouTube

Looking for readymade clips from this and similar sites is not only potentially time saving but can also provide teachers with ideas that they might not have had before searching the sites. The large quantity of materials, also including those materials that are not suitable for English lessons, might also make it difficult to find the right clips. There are many more portals, some of them being specifically designed for educational purposes. Some portals for searching for and creating podcasts have already been referred to in chapter 3.3. Table 4.2 introduces a few more such sites.

Videojug	videojug. com	A whole set of "how to ..." videos that serve as demonstrations for all different aspects of life, such as arts and crafts, different types of sports, cooking, job interviews or networking.
Podomatic	podomatic. com	Portal with free podcasts sorted into categories, such as arts, business, education, hobbies or health.
English as a second lang- uage podcast	eslpod.com	A commercial site with podcasts and additional materials that are designed for individualized language learning
Educational Video-Podcasts	teachers.tv	A portal with educational videos to be used in schools within the UK. If started from the site, the videos cannot be watched outside the UK; quite a few of the videos have been uploaded onto YouTube though.

Table 4.2: Portals with podcasts

Portals with literature

At the time of writing most books, short stories and poems are still bought in print but the emergence of affordable ebook readers already raises the question of what part in the market ebooks will play in the future. Literature can already be downloaded for a fee. Literature with a small l, i.e. texts which are not regarded as high standard literature but still offer an authentic look at a particular culture and are of use in lessons (see Thaler 2008), can also be found online, often for free. Literature with a small l would include newspaper articles, cartoons, jokes or lyrics for songs. For some of those only viewing the texts online will be legal, while printing and distributing them in the class is often illegal, which means that in some cases it might be advisable to use the digital versions.

literature online

Cartoons & Comics
Glasbergen (glasbergen.com) Glasbergen is a cartoonist who creates cartoons for all purposes of life. The cartoons can be viewed online but cannot be copied for free.
Madam & Eve (mg.co.za/madameve/all) Madam & Eve are the South African white lady and her domestic worker – the cartoons introduce current issues in South Africa in a humorous and sometimes quite sarcastic way.
Zapiro (zapiro.com) Zapiro is also a cartoonist who publishes in the South African Mail & Guardian, is well known for his dramatic cartoons on South African politics and history
Comics.com (comics.com) A big portal with links to different types of comics from the United Feature Syndicate which can be viewed online for free.

Jokes
Aha Jokes (ahajokes.com) **Lots of Jokes** (lotsofjokes.com) **The internet TESL Journal** – Jokes for Teachers (iteslj.org/c/jokes.html)
Jokes sites, most of which are more suitable for the teacher as some of the sites contain contents that are not appropriate for younger learners.

Table 4.3: Websites with literature

Portals for Self Study

Screenshot 4.2: The BBC Learning English Portal

A lot of the resources listed above can be used by the learners themselves during their private study or when working on tasks set by the teacher. There are many portals that have been especially developed for learners of English as a foreign or second language however.

A large portal in itself is the *BBC Learning English* part of the BBC website. With adapted and annotated versions of news reports, different series which can be read, viewed or listened to regularly, interactive quizzes, materials for skills development, vocabulary and grammar training, a forum and a lot more, the site can be seen as a giant free of charge training site. Also, it is a portal that provides students with important current information in an interesting and easily digestible way.

Likewise the BBC Bitesize portal could be used by learners of English. The Bitesize portal links to interactive training sites for students in England who prepare for their GCSEs, their exams in year 11. Because some of the materials might be quite complex from a linguistic point of view and convey cultural beliefs that lend themselves to discussions in class, the use of those sites might also be directed by the teacher.

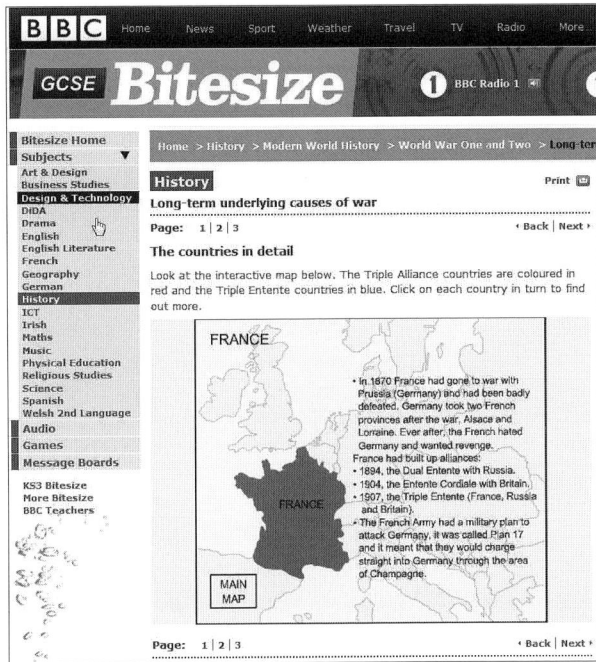

Screenshot 4.3: BBC Bitesize contents for History

Independent study sites · There is vast number of other portals, focusing on grammar, vocabulary, collocations and also the development of listening, speaking, reading or writing skills. Table 4.4 includes just a selection of those sites. For a good overview of free portals on the net see the Virtual Language Centre of the University of Duisburg-Essen which links to many web pages with free interactive contents.

Learn English (British Council) learnenglish.britishcouncil.org learnenglishkids.british-council.org	The Learn English sites of the British Council are big portals with free materials for individual study – there are podcasts and video podcasts for supporting listening skills with full vocabulary support and accompanying interactive tasks, columns with articles on British food, vocabulary and grammar exercises, materials for business English, preparatory exams (e.g. for the IELTS) and an online community. The kids site contains games and listening activities, e.g. with stories for younger learners.
Dave's ESL cafe eslcafe.com	Dave's ESL Cafe is a portal for teachers and learners alike. For students there are many resources, such as grammar lessons or lists of idioms and phrasal verbs as well as interactive quizzes on areas, such as Geography or on grammatical phenomena.
Virtual Language Center – VLC (uni-due.de/anglistik/applied_linguistics_didactics/vlc)	The Virtual Language Centre of the University of Duisburg-Essen provides many links to other self study sites, to online resources, such as online newspapers and to reference tools, such as dictionaries but there are also online exercises that have been developed especially for the site.
BBC Learning English bbc.co.uk/worldservice/learningenglish **Bitesize** bbc.co.uk/schools/gcsebitesize	The BBC Learning English service has already been described in detail above. The GCSE bitesize site offers structured practice for the GCSE exams for all subjects; thus, teachers might be able to pick out study materials for specific literary texts or for content based instruction, e.g. in Biology or History. Likewise those materials can be used for students' independent explorations on a topic.

Table 4.4: Portals for self-access learning

For more information on the so-called tutor function of the computer see chapter 7 which is dedicated to the history, the classification and the use of tutorial courseware.

Teacher Development: Portals with information and links

Once teachers are fully trained, they are normally by themselves in the classroom. Further training is done through training days and through the exchange of ideas with colleagues but on the whole teachers in Germany have to look out for new ideas and help themselves in order to develop further. There are a lot of materials on the web for ongoing training and inspiration which can provide teachers with useful information, lesson plans, tips, hints and materials for lessons. Some of the portals described below are governmental initiatives, others sites of interest groups or innovative teachers who have been active in the field of teaching with and without technology for years. Table 4.5 provides brief descriptions of a number of informative and educational sites.

Information on teaching English with computers

Bildungsserver bildungsserver.de/ learn-line.nrw.de/ schule-bw.de/	The online portals belong to government authorities offer guided help for all subjects, often with link lists to online resources.
Fremdsprachenunterricht in der Informationsgesell-schaft (Donath) schule.de/englisch/reinhard additional new site: donathwebzwei.word-press.com/	Reinhard Donath is an extremely experienced and successful secondary school teacher who has pioneered many uses of New Media in schools in Germany. His sites provide input on how to go about using, e.g. blogs or webquests in English lessons, it provides his own examples of his former uses of media and also a link list to more best practice examples as well as other useful sites.
ICT4LT ict4lt.org/	ICT4LT (ICT for language teachers) is a site run by Graham Davies, one of the most renowned figures in the field of CALL. Here, again, one can find a lot of "how to ..." information, very good background information with references to research and study books but also a glossary of ICT related terms and many samples of good practice.
Lehrer Online lehrer-online.de/	Lehrer online is an online portal belonging to the German company lo-net that offers many online articles on how to make use of New Media in lessons as well as concrete practical articles on projects.
The Internet TESL Journal iteslj.org/	The internet TESL (Teaching English as a Second Language) journal provides articles for teacher development as well as resources for teachers.

Teaching English (British Council) britishcouncil.org/ learning-teaching-english- gateway	The 'Think' section on the British Council Teaching English site contains articles on how to teach English. The site also contains lesson plans, resources and many teaching ideas in general under the 'Try' section.
Teachit teachit.co.uk	The Teachit site is full of teaching resources, training materials, and more. Only registered members can edit the resources they found, however, and one needs a paid membership in order to be able to get all the fully editable resources, including the PowerPoint and Smartboard files for example.

Table 4.5: Portals on English Language Teaching Methodology

4.4 Reference Tools

What kinds of tools do you use as a reference when you are, for example, writing texts in English?

Reference tools online are valuable for teachers and learners alike, inside and outside of lessons. They are of help when one is looking for specific information concerning language or content matters. The most commonly employed reference tools are dictionaries, thesauri, encyclopaedia, to some extent concordancing programmes and now also, regretfully, free translation tools.

All these tools are most handy during writing or reading processes on the computer as this is when they can be integrated best. The possibilities for using them are too great to mention them all. Although some training might be helpful for learners, they should be applied in a way that resembles as much as possible their use in professional life.

Online Dictionaries

Using leo & co   Being able to refer to a dictionary as a strategy for learning, checking and editing work is a basic skill for language learners as it gives them the opportunity to work and carry on learning independently. As it is such an important skill, its development is a stated aim of all curricula, even for English at primary level. In addition to printed versions and digital ones on CD ROM, various online dictionaries have been developed and probably even more will be developed in the future. For publishers the advantage of dictionaries online is that changes can be made quickly without having to publish a completely new version. For users the advantage is that they can access online dictionaries without having to purchase a book or CD-ROM that they need to carry around with them.

Although the information the free online dictionaries provide is often not as well structured and thorough as in the bigger printed versions, they can help to find the information needed in a given situation. Features shared by the most common bilingual online dictionaries, such as dict.cc or leo.org, is the search function for translating words and idioms as well as the opportunity to listen to the right pronunciation. Both, dict.cc and leo.org are, at the time of writing, growing into increasingly comprehensive sites with many different options to follow. Also, their use in lessons nowadays is not dependent on the number of computers available in the classroom anymore, as students and teachers are able to use these sites via apps for smartphones (also see chapter 10). See table 4.6 for a list of some currently popular online dictionaries.

Leo Leo.org	Free bilingual dictionary, initiated by the TU Munich, that does not only translate German-English, English-German but also from and into many other languages.
Dict.cc Dict.cc	Another free online German-English, English-German dictionary with an interactive vocabulary trainer for registered users.
Little explorers enchantedlearning.com/ Dictionary	A picture dictionary that is especially of use for young learners. There is a monolingual version with pictures and definitions as well as a bilingual English-German, German-English version with pictures. So far the dictionary can be used for free, but to get access to the other Enchanted Learning Resources one has to register and pay.
Pons online pons.eu/dict/search	Free bilingual online dictionary for many languages, not only German-English, English-German. The search results include phrasal verbs and idioms. There is a machine generated pronunciation tool for the search word.
Merriam Webster Merriam-webster.com	Monolingual dictionary with definitions, examples of the word in context, etymological information, synonyms and related terms as suggestions for a new search.

Table 4.6: A Collection of Popular Online Dictionaries

Thesauri

A comprehensive thesaurus is already part of word processing programmes, for example, so for a lot of queries this might suffice. Some online thesauri, e.g. thesaurus.com, offer more comprehensive information, such as a definition of the search word and additional notes on how the use of the word differs from the use of near synonyms. Thesauri are, or probably should be, used by everyone who writes texts on the computer. It can help avoid repetitive language use and can thus lead to a more elaborate style of writing.

Online thesauri

Name	Description
Thesaurus.com Thesaurus.com	Includes a definition of the search word, an extensive list of synonyms (with links to entries for these words), and explanations on the use of these words
Merriam Webster Merriam-webster.com	Includes a definition of the search word, a list of synonyms, a list of related words, phrases with similar meaning and a list of antonyms

Table 4.7: Two commonly used online thesauri

Again, most of these tools are available as apps for the different smartphone operating systems, so that mobile phones could be used in a very productive way during project work or writing in class.

Concordancing programmes

Research into authentic language use

Concordancing programmes are tools that search corpora for entries. Corpora are collections of texts, be it of written or spoken language. One might either want to search corpora that one has put together oneself, such as a collection of newspaper articles on a given topic, a collection of blog entries, text written by one and the same author or, for example, lyrics of songs from the 50s. Alternatively one could search one of the big, well-known corpora. Big corpora that one could search are, for example, the British National Corpus BNC, the Australian Corpus of English ACE or the American National Corpus ANC. The biggest of those established corpora of written and spoken English is the Bank of English with about 524 million words. The corpus is based on authentic language e.g. from newspaper articles, books or transcribed speech.

One might want to search a corpus in order to find out, for example, what the most frequent words are or how often and in which contexts specific words are used. Concordancing programmes in connection with corpora of language open up the option of doing research into authentic language use. Searching corpora thus offers us quite a different view on language than prescriptive grammars, phrase books or selective dictionaries and is often referred to as Data Driven Learning. If the right tasks are given, Concordancing tools facilitate an explorative approach and can also serve as a quick and simple reference tool, should one not be sure about the use of a word or expression.

One of the most well-known online concordancers is the Harper Collins one (Harper Collins Wordbanks). A trial version can be tested for 30 days, other than that a licence has to be purchased.

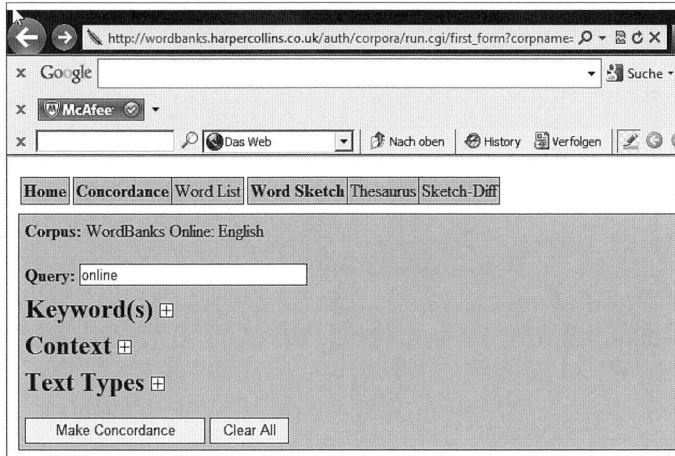

Screenshot 4.4: The Harper Collins Wordbanks Online

There is also the British National Corpus that can be searched with a trial version of an online concordancer.

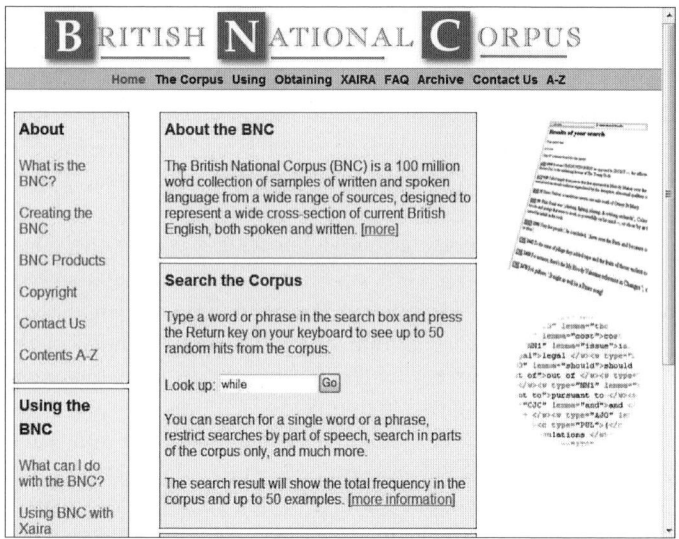

Screenshot 4.5: The Sample Concordancer of the BNC

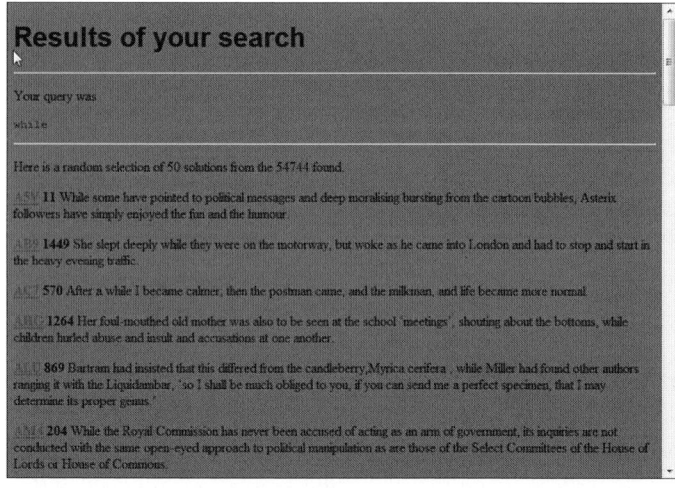

Screenshot 4.6: Search results (concs) for the term "while"

Online sample concordancers are sufficient for many types of research into authentic use of English. There are also many offline concordancers that will search any corpus that is available (see corpus-linguistics.info). For the investigation of real language use in lessons it might often make more sense to use concordancers as a teaching tool to provide the students with the search results, i.e. the concordances. In screenshot 4.6, for example, the concordances for the word "while" can be used for explorative grammar and lexis work, i.e. the students can try to find out by themselves in which functions "while" is used in these search results.

The real charm in using concordancers is in posing one's own research questions. This kind of use should be the aim if teachers introduce the work with concordancers in their English classes. Only when students know how to read the results, will it make sense to encourage the use of concordancers as a tool, for example for supporting the writing process.

Google, in this context sometimes referred to as a "quick and dirty concordancer" (Chinnery 2008: 4), is often used in the same way as concordancers are. If unsure about certain expressions or words, many people consult search engines in order to find out about the contexts in which the search word or expression is used on the internet. In contrast to the entries in the big corpora, these also contain many unedited and also sometimes incorrect English phrases used by non native speakers, i.e. one always has to double check the sources before trusting the results. For more information on searching the web with search engines see chapter 5.

Translation Tools

Translation tools claim to be able to translate words, sentences and even whole texts into another language. They are very popular in the business and also the private sector, in the latter taking the form of free online versions, the so-called free translators. Although the tools have improved throughout the years, there are clear limits as to what they can achieve. Translation is a very skilled profession for which one does not only need an extremely good command of at least two languages but also good knowledge of the target culture, cultural conventions and the context the translation is for. We know that even for a simple list of words they will not be able to get one correct translation as there is not a one-to-one translation of concepts into the other language. When it comes to words in context, complex syntax and cultural

The art of translating

aspects, it becomes a real challenge for these programmes to transfer the structures and ideas into the target language correctly and it will be even more difficult to express subtle connotations.

The quality of free translators

One might argue that if translation tools are applied in business contexts, students will need help to be able to work with them. Instead of encouraging extensive use within lessons, however, teachers should instead demonstrate what kinds of skills and knowledge are required in order to interpret the results correctly. Students could, for example, type in culturally loaded texts into one of those tools in order to get an insight into the potential and limitations of free translation tools.

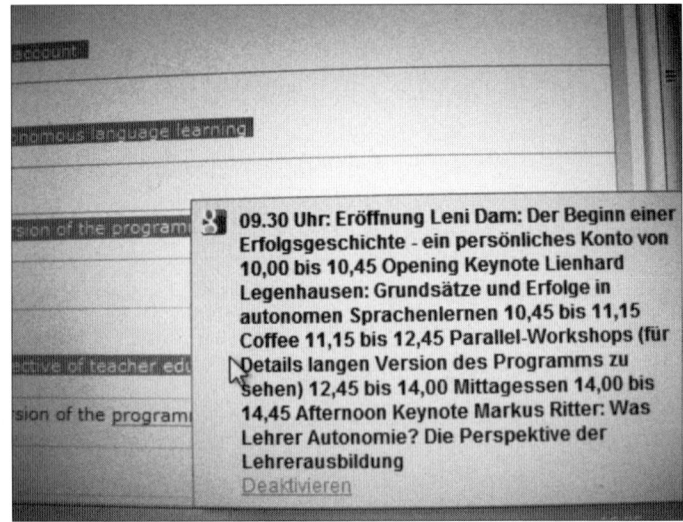

Screenshot 4.7: The automatic translation service of Google

The translation that is shown in screenshot 4.7 already makes clear some of the limitations of translation tools, in this case the Google translator. While some expressions are translated correctly and while it is still possible to guess what the translated text is about, it does by no means result in a correct German version. To take it a step further, you might want to type a short passage of a literary text into the translation tool.

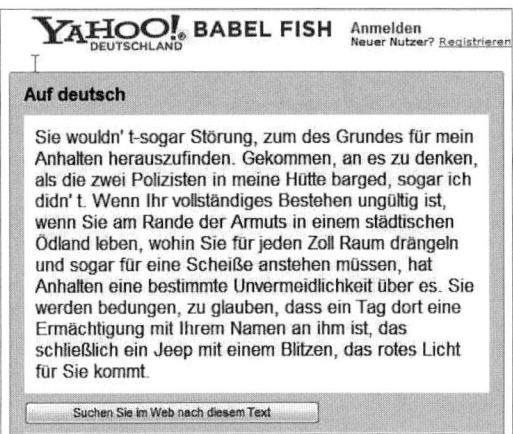

YAHOO! BABEL FISH DEUTSCHLAND

Anmelden
Neuer Nutzer? Registrieren

Auf deutsch

Sie wouldn' t-sogar Störung, zum des Grundes für mein Anhalten herauszufinden. Gekommen, an es zu denken, als die zwei Polizisten in meine Hütte barged, sogar ich didn' t. Wenn Ihr vollständiges Bestehen ungültig ist, wenn Sie am Rande der Armuts in einem städtischen Ödland leben, wohin Sie für jeden Zoll Raum drängeln und sogar für eine Scheiße anstehen müssen, hat Anhalten eine bestimmte Unvermeidlichkeit über es. Sie werden bedungen, zu glauben, dass ein Tag dort eine Ermächtigung mit Ihrem Namen an ihm ist, das schließlich ein Jeep mit einem Blitzen, das rotes Licht für Sie kommt.

Suchen Sie im Web nach diesem Text

Screenshot 4.8: A Babelfish translation of text excerpt from English into German

If you read the German translation that Babelfish produced for the extract above (see screenshot 4.8) you would not necessarily guess that it is supposed to be the German version of an extract from Vikas Swarup's *Slumdog Millionaire*. Here is, for the sake of comparability, the extract that we typed in:

> They wouldn't even bother to find out the reason for my arrest. Come to think of it, when the two constables barged into my hut, even I didn't. When your whole existence is illegal, when you live on the brink of penury in an urban wasteland where you jostle for every inch of space and have to queue even for a shit, arrest has a certain inevitability about it. You are conditioned to believe that one day there will be a warrant with your name on it, that eventually a jeep with a flashing red light will come for you.
>
> (Swarup 2005: 12)

This is complex and rich language which, as the translation shows, cannot easily be translated into another language by a machine. So although one can also appreciate this as the result of complex processes, it is by no means good enough to be a real help when it comes to writing texts. And even if students just wanted to use translation tools for the sake of comprehension rather than the production of an elaborate text, they would hardly be successful here.

Online Encyclopaedias

Wikipedia as a reference

The big well-known encyclopaedias in libraries would nowadays grow dusty if it wasn't for traditionalists and devoted librarians who are convinced of the superiority of the printed text. Nowadays there are Wikipedia and other online encyclopaedias that make teachers and lecturers at university despair because their students would not bother to check the information that they found online in a real book. Wikipedia, the most well known online encyclopaedia, can be added to by anyone who is motivated to contribute and is constantly worked on by many people who may or may not be experts in a particular field (for more information on the functions of wikis see chapter 8.3).

This is the reason why many people warn against uncritically using Wikipedia as a resource. While one has to say that using any kind of information unchecked is something to warn against, Wikipedia as a source is not as bad as its reputation would suggest. Experts have compared entries in Wikipedia with entries in the Encyclopaedia Britannica, the most well known and comprehensive British encyclopaedia, and they found that there are almost as many mistakes in the traditional encyclopaedia as there are in Wikipedia (Giles 2005). In the same fashion the magazine Stern mandated a research company to find out whether the online version of *Der Brockhaus* was better than Wikipedia (Stern. de 2007). In this study Wikipedia beat the more traditional dictionary by far. One of Wikipedia's biggest strengths is that it is up to date. But it is also no less correct than the Brockhaus – at least not in the 50 entries that were looked at. Those tests were carried out back in 2005 and 2007. In the meantime Wikipedia has grown and has attracted more and more specialists as well as lay persons. That in itself acts as a large quality check, simply because there are so many potential editors out there who will set things straight if necessary. Wikipedia's credibility is also checked by an editing team that encourages potential contributors to improve articles that they regard as poor and who also warn that an article might be deleted if not changed in due time. Training students to look out for signs of credibility and encouraging them to crosscheck with other sources will certainly still be necessary but quoting from Wikipedia is not necessarily seen as a no-go area anymore. So, as we write, Wikipedia is undergoing a big change concerning its credibility.

For beginner learners it might be helpful to use the "Simple English" version of Wikipedia that is specifically written for children and learners of English and encourages all authors to use simple words and grammar. There is also a kids version of the Encyclopaedia Britannica online with an option to search the kids or the teens version of entries. Just like the version for adults, the free online kids version only provides the first couple of sentences of an entry.

4.5 Focus on Research

How reliant are you on reference tools when you are writing texts in English? Does their use really have an impact on the quality of your text?

Recent research has focused on the effects of using reference tools in EFL lessons. Koo (2006) has tested the effect of using reference tools for writing texts. Koo asked her Korean ESL learners to paraphrase a newspaper article. The reference tools which were used were dictionaries, thesauri and a corpus that learners could search with a concordancer. Reference tools certainly do play a bigger role in supporting writing rather than speaking skills in general, as only writing really allows the time for editing. Thus, using those reference tools in the context of writing can be seen as an authentic usage. The task of paraphrasing a newspaper article that was used during the research is not authentic but aimed at training students in editing their own texts, i.e. making them linguistically more diverse. It was also meant to be training for using information from other texts without repeating the parts referred to word by word.

Using reference tools for writing

Koo found out that those learners who combined the use of the two reference tools when looking for a specific aspect were especially successful. On the whole, she found that the application of reference tools had improved learners' accuracy in writing as well as their confidence as they had access to authentic linguistic resources to back up their choices (2006: 1, 183-185).

4.6 Classroom Ideas

How can the use of the resources described above help to create more learner-centred lessons?

A lot of the resources described in this chapter lend themselves to traditional classroom work, i.e. the analysis of texts, listening comprehension or viewing tasks etc. Thus, most of the materials can be used in a predominantly teacher centred lesson as well as in more student centred, e.g. task based or also project based, lessons. As already outlined in this chapter, there are quite a few video clips online for demonstration or other purposes. If there is the option of projecting a film in the classroom, the demonstration of a shopping dialogue, for example, can be used as add on in class, to give a full professional model of what such a conversation can be like. The dialogue can first be explored through comprehension tasks, before it is then used as a basis for students' own creative work.

Screenshot 4.9: Conversation Tips from a Peason Longman language training clip (taken from: http://www.youtube.com/watch?v=bk5ukX ooGqQ)

For more grown up students a "how to" video concerning job interviews can be helpful for awareness raising either prior to their own trial interviews or after their first trial round. The guidelines provided in the video can be discussed in class and can also be used as guideline for students' own role plays in class.

Screenshot 4.10: A shot from a how to video for job interviews http://www.videojug.com/film/how-to-perform-effectively-in-a-job-interview

For a more student centred approach the described materials should be available to students for independent exploration, either in groups or by themselves, e.g. through the use of several laptops or in a computer room. The reference tools referred to in this chapter will also be available, either on the computer or on students' smartphones and can be used for supporting any kind of follow-up work.

While the handling of all reference tools requires some training, the use of concordancers, or rather the analysis of the results, the concordances, is certainly very demanding. Doing research with concordances requires a good knowledge of what one is looking for and which search words will lead to the best results. A lot of work with concordancers will be done with a focus on language form, be it as a reference tool when it comes to using idiomatic language or for exploring any kind of linguistic research question. The applicability of concordancers exceeds the exploration of purely linguistic issues however. The analysis of language use can be valuable for many other disciplines, such as psychology or the analysis of literature. In connection with the analysis of literature concordancers can be of help for finding out about an author's style of writing or also for characterizations of characters, for example. By looking at the verbs or adjectives that are used in connection with a person's name one can deduce what kind of person he or she might be.

Analysing literature with concordancers

When analysing the concordances created for the search word "Alice" with the Concordancer of the Victorian Literary Studies Archive (victorian.lang.nagoya-u.ac.jp/concordance) that includes a sample of literary texts in its corpus, we can draw a lot of conclusions about Alice the well-known character in the book *Alice in Wonderland*. Concordances are a real help in that they condense large pieces of information. In this way they can also serve as a basis for awareness raising, e.g. concerning what kinds of information help us to portray a character. In addition to a purely analytical use it might also serve as a preparation for more creative work, e.g. prior to staging Alice in Wonderland with a class or drama club.

```
Carroll, Lewis : Alice's Adventures in Wonderland
Total text lines : 3353
Total word count : 27338
Query result : 398

     1:              ALICE'S ADVENTURES IN WONDERLAND (1865) LEWIS CARROLL CHAPTER I Down the
     8:    I Down the Rabbit-Hole Alice was beginning to get very tired of sitting by her sister on the bank,
    11:    the use of a book,' thought Alice 'without pictures or conversation?' So she was considering in her own
    20:    remarkable in that; nor did Alice think it so VERY much out of the way to hear the Rabbit say to itself,
    26:    at it, and then hurried on, Alice started to her feet, for it flashed across her mind that she had never
    33:    In another moment down went Alice after it, never once considering how in the world she was to get out
    37:    down, so suddenly that Alice had not a moment to think about stopping herself before she found
    53:    past it. 'Well!' thought Alice to herself, 'after such a fall as this, I shall think nothing of
    62:    I think -- ' (for, you see, Alice had learnt several things of this sort in her lessons in the schoolroom,
    67:    Longitude I've got to?' ( Alice had no idea what Latitude was, or Longitude either, but thought they
    82:    was nothing else to do, so Alice soon began talking again. 'Dinah'll miss me very much to-night, I
    88:    bats, I wonder?' And here Alice began to get rather sleepy, and went on saying to herself, in a dreamy
    98:    and the fall was over. Alice was not a bit hurt, and she jumped up on to her feet in a moment: she
   102:    to be lost: away went Alice like the wind, and was just in time to hear it say, as it turned a
   109:    were all locked; and when Alice had been all the way down one side and up the other, trying every door,
   115:    a tiny golden key, and Alice's first thought was that it might belong to one of the doors of the
   123:    great delight it fitted! Alice opened the door and found that it led into a small passage, not much
   129:    go through,' thought poor Alice, 'it would be of very little use without my shoulders. Oh, how I wish I
   132:    had happened lately, that Alice had begun to think that very few things indeed were really impossible.
   139:    was not here before,' said Alice.) and round the neck of the bottle was a paper label, with the words
   143:    me,' but the wise little Alice was not going to do THAT in a hurry. 'No, I'll look first,' she said,
```

Screenshot 4.11: Concs for the search word Alice

Tasks

1. Choose three portals for newspapers and/or TV channels. Jot down the main features and the features that impressed you most. Be prepared to talk about those portals in class.
2. Browse any of the portals with video clips. Find one clip that you would like to use in class. Also develop first ideas of how you could use it.
3. Just like in task 2, find one piece of literature that you would like to use with your students online. Be prepared to talk about the reasons for your choice.
4. Explore any of the named independent study sites. Be able to talk about the following aspects

Site	
Target Group	
Features	
Comments (potential for classroom work, advantages, disadvantages, ...)	

5. Choose one of the teacher development sites. Find an article on a topic you are interested in but not familiar with as yet. Read it, print it out and bring it to class for further discussion.

6. Use any combination of reference tools in order to translate the following sentence into English: (Hinsichtlich einer Gesamtwürdigung ist Frau M. trotz der genannten Schwächen zugute zu halten, dass sie sich bemüht hat, das komplexe Feld der Fehleranalyse und die damit verbundenen linguistischen Traditionen theoretisch zu erfassen und empirisch-praktisch auf Lernerdaten anzuwenden.)

7. Reflect on the process of translating the sentence in task 6 as well as on your general experience with reference tools. In how far are your personal findings in line with the research results referred to in this chapter?

8. Choose any kind of online resource (can be the same as in task 1, 2 or 3) and develop a meaningful task around it. Think about what you would do prior to using the resource, what kinds of tasks your students would get while working with the resource and what kind of follow-up work could make sense.

WEB RESEARCH | 5

5.1 Overview

What are your strategies for searching the net? Do you think they are effective?

The importance of teaching students how to find and evaluate information is a traditional educational goal and was of importance long before the internet became accessible for the general public. In former times searching books in the library might have been the main focus of interest. As a lot work by experts is still only available in print, this certainly is a key skill and will be for a while. A lot of academic publications and reference works are (also) available online nowadays, and information that used to be only found in library buildings is now also – and in some cases – exclusively available on the web. As the web is the first place where many people look out for information, the ability to use the net safely and efficiently is becoming increasingly important.

Normalization of Web Research

In classroom situations web research is often introduced through so-called *WebQuests* which are the subject of chapter 5.2. Most people, when they are looking for something on the web, use search engines. In chapter 5.3 we will explore the different uses of search engines and their potential for English lessons. Chapters 5.4 and 5.5 will focus on research that has been done in the field and on ideas for the classroom. Thus, while chapter 4 focused on specific resources that can be useful for language teaching and learning, this chapter will mainly focus on procedures and tools for searching the web. For information on how to publish documents on the web see chapter 8 on social software.

5.2 WebQuests

Using the name of the term as a clue, what might the aim of a WebQuest be?

WebQuests as introduction to Web Research

As the term suggests, someone who is doing a WebQuest is seeking to find something on the web. A WebQuest is a strategy, developed and set by trainers and teachers, who usually decide on the aims, the potential outcomes, the tasks, the procedures and often also on the sites that are to be searched as well. Thus, it can be regarded as a method of training learners to find relevant information on websites and to use it for their purposes.

The idea of a WebQuest as strategy for teaching in schools is not new at all. The term was coined by Bernie Dodge in 1995 and was defined as "an inquiry-oriented activity in which some or all of the information that learners interact with comes from resources on the web" (Dodge 1995: 1). The information students need in order to find the information they are looking for is often provided on a Website that is created for the WebQuest. A successful WebQuest will at least consist of the following parts (Dodge 1995: 2; screenshots and information in brackets added):

1) An **introduction** that sets the stage and provides some background information.

Structure of WebQuests

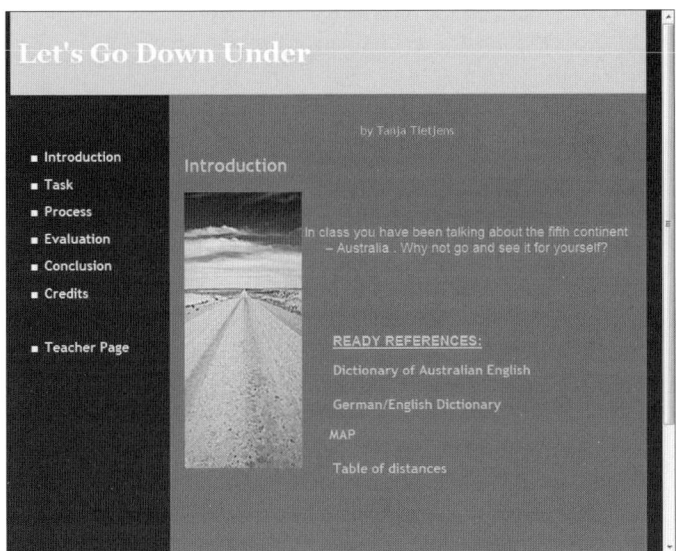

Screenshot 5.1: The introductory page of a WebQuest on Australia created by Tietjens (taken from: http://questgarden.com/54/38/3/071117033846/index.htm))

2) A **task** that is doable and interesting.

Screenshot 5.2: The task site of the Australia WebQuest

3) A set of **information sources** needed to complete the task. Many (though not necessarily all) of the resources are embedded in the WebQuest document itself as anchors pointing to information on the World Wide Web. Information sources might include web documents, experts available via e-mail or realtime conferencing, searchable databases on the net, and books and other documents physically available in the learner's setting. Because pointers to resources are included, the learner is not left to wander through webspace completely adrift. (In the sample WebQuest provided the only sources that are provided by the teacher are the ones that can be seen on the introductory page. All other pieces of information will (apparently) have to be found independently by the students).

4) A description of the **process** the learners should go through in accomplishing the task. The process should be broken down into clearly described steps.

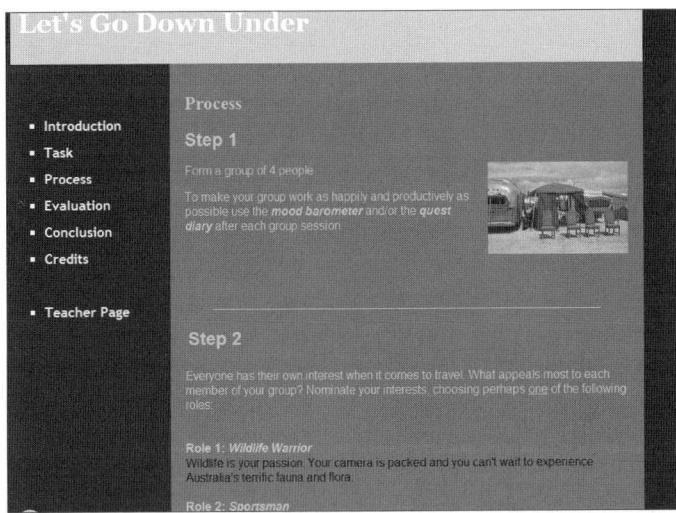

Screenshot 5.3: The process site of the Australia WebQuest

5) **Guidance** on how to organize the information acquired. This could be guiding questions, or directions to complete organizational frameworks such as timelines, concept maps, or cause-and-effect diagrams. (In the sample WebQuest on Australia the set outcomes, i.e. the PowerPoint presentation and the travel brochure and their knowledge on what these outcomes could look like serve as a guideline for students (see snapshot 5.2)).

6) A **conclusion** that brings closure to the quest, reminds the learners about what they have learned, and perhaps encourages them to extend the experience into other domains.

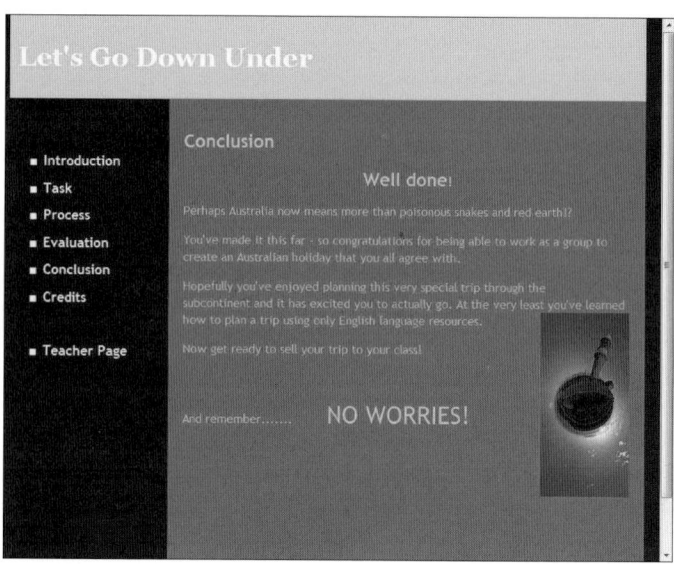

Screenshot 5.4: The Conclusion of the Australia WebQuest

Transparent parameter for evaluation

Additional desirable features of WebQuests are descriptors on how students' work is going to be evaluated (see snapshot 5.5). This will help students to structure their process (see point 4) and also to draw a conclusion regarding the process and the outcome of the WebQuest (see point 6). This also means that students, parents and fellow teachers will get a better idea of how this kind of project work is graded. This is helpful in order to be able to justify a project that exceeds a small number of lessons. Even though the aims that are achieved in a successful WebQuest are in line with the curricula and are certainly valuable for students' future lives, there might be severe criticism if the outcomes of such a WebQuest cannot be assessed properly. In the long run this transparency regarding the criteria of assessment alongside regular monitoring of the process contributes to students' ability to work in groups responsibly and independently.

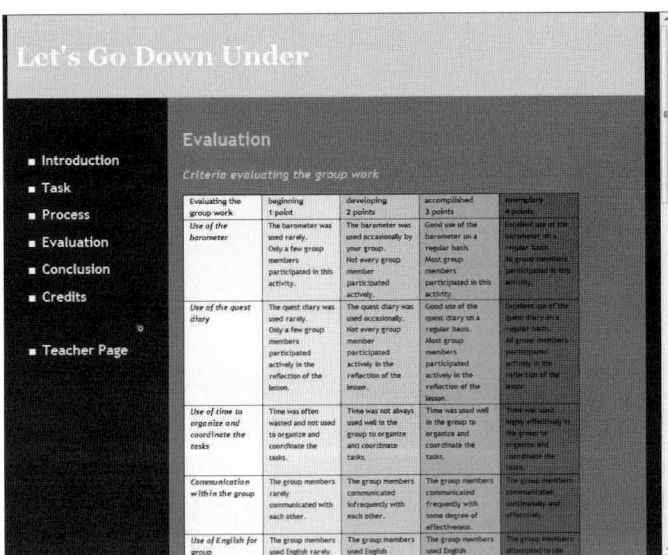

Screenshot 5.5: The evaluation grid of the Australia WebQuest

WebQuests can take many different forms. They could only last one lesson or, like the sample WebQuest above, several lessons. The most important feature for the quality of a WebQuest is the type of tasks one sets. Tasks which aim at helping students to really look into something in order to gain deeper insights into an issue, e.g. by analyzing or comparing information or by looking for proof for or against a thesis, certainly have a bigger potential for higher order processing of information than a sheer fact finding task.

The quality of tasks

According to March (2003) the quality of a WebQuest can be judged by three Rs: A good WebQuest is real, rich and relevant. He claims that some web-based activities might look like WebQuests but don't require any higher order thinking as students do not need to transform the given information in order to create a meaningful product.

"Real" WebQuests

In the example above the students have to create a travel brochure and a PowerPoint presentation on their chosen travel routes on the basis of the information they find online and also have to present their results in front of the class. Also, students have to be collaborative in order to be able to agree on a plan.

Still, from March's perspective, the WebQuest would probably be considered to be rather superficial as students only do fact finding online, they only get to see what prospective tourists are meant to see and could, if they wanted to, just copy and paste or summarize blurbs they find online. So, although the activities might be regarded as good communicative tasks, the input and the tasks are not rich and relevant in that they don't necessarily stir students' imagination or question their belief system. Thus they do not automatically provoke higher order thinking (March 2003). On March's site BestWebQuests and Dodge's sites *A WebQuest about WebQuests* and *WebQuest.org* (see table 5.1) one can find links to example WebQuests that they regard as real, rich and relevant.

Information about
WebQuests

URL	Description
webquest.org	The most comprehensive site on Web-Quests with a vast amount of information, e.g. on the history of WebQuests, related ideas, help for creating Webquests and concrete examples. Created by Bernie Dodge.
Bestwebquests.com	Tom March's website with selected WebQuests for different subjects, which have been rated.
A WebQuest about WebQuests http://webquest.sdsu.edu/webquestwebquest-es.html	Bernie Dodge's training site on Web-Quests on which one learns about WebQuests by working on one in a group. There are example WebQuests on the site which can be viewed for information purposes as well.
schule.de/englisch/daf_web-quest	Donath's page about WebQuests with definitions, descriptions of procedures and stages and concrete examples
Lehrer-online.de	There are several articles on WebQuests on the Lehrer Online portal. One of the training sites is a WebQuest that helps teachers to learn how to create a Web-Quest themselves.

e-teaching.org	Here you find introductory articles, links and very useful information on how to use WebQuests for tests.
questgarden.com	A platform with information on Web-Quests, sample WebQuests and ready-made WebQuests for teachers who register and pay. Also, there is a tool that can be used for creating one's own WebQuest.

Table 5.1: A collection of informative sites on WebQuests

WebQuests cannot only be used for developing skills and gaining knowledge, they can also be used for e-tests. In this case the focus is on testing problem solving skills and the ability to extract relevant information from the internet (for more information see e-teaching.org).

For creating WebQuests themselves teachers do need a bit of time and computer literacy. But with social software, i.e. online tools that allow for quick and easy publication of materials on the internet, creating WebQuests has also become easier. A lot of the WebQuests that can be found as examples on Donath's site, (see table 5.1) have been created with the help of blogging software (see chapter 8.4). The sample WebQuest presented in this chapter has been created with Questgarden, an "online authoring tool, community and hosting service that is designed to make it easier and quicker to create a high quality WebQuest" (Questgarden 2010).

Creating WebQuests

5.3 Search Engines

What is your favourite search engine and how often do you use it?

Using search engines has become so wide-spread that even a new verb has been generated for searching information on the web with the help of, at the time of writing, *the* most common search engine, Google. An equivalent for "to google" has quickly entered many different languages, with *googeln* in German, *googler* in French, *guguru* in Japanese or *googlować* in Polish.

Google:
Facts & Figures

The search engine that has, over the last decade, gained such world-wide acceptance, was founded in the USA in 1998 by students Larry Page and Sergey Brin. One assumption about why Google is so popular is the very simple design and the clear structure of the site. Another reason is the technique with which the web is searched. Instead of just counting the number of times an item is mentioned on a site, Google uses a set of complex routines in order to find out the number of links that refer to the different sites in question and also checks the popularity of sites in order to find and display the most popular hits. Also, the contents of the page and neighbouring pages are taken into consideration in order to find the most relevant matches for the search query.

The search is done with such ease and speed that one might fail to think about the effort and energy that is used in order to run the search engine. At the time of writing there are about 10,000 employees working for Google (for updated information see: google.de/corporate/facts), and all the queries are only answered at such speed because there is a vast number of Google servers all over the world. Experts argue about the amount of carbon dioxide that is set free for one search, with one of the most extreme claims being that two searches use up as much energy as boiling a cup of water with a kettle (Boulton 2009). Although one can claim that the same will be true for all servers and offers on the web, it seems quite striking, how much workforce and technology is needed to keep one offer running.

Trusting Google:
Some critical
thoughts

Learning about and keeping in mind how the search results get onto our computer screen is not only useful for environmental reasons but also for developing learners' media literacy. The use of Google is for free but Google is a company that has to make a profit. Thus, a lot of the links shown together with the search results lead to sites of companies which have paid for this display. There is also a whole market emerging with experts who know about Google's search algorithm and who offer companies a service of composing sites that will appear as high as possible on the Google lists. Thus, trusting Google is like trusting any other company to give you the best possible information and should certainly not be done without a critical eye. Google has already lost some of its reputation because of Google Streetview which enables users to get a full 3D impression of streets and houses. As a result the question of privacy protection and of how much data Google stores has been raised again. Lessons on how to use Google or any other kind of search engine should thus ideally be accompanied by a closer look at functions and terms & conditions. For a list of additional well-known search engines see table 5.2.

Search Engine	URL
Google	google.com, www.google.de, google.co.uk,..
Yahoo	de.yahoo.com/
MSN	msn.com/; de.msn.com/
Bing	Bing.com
Ask.com	Ask.com

Table 5.2: The currently most well-known search engines

Functions of Search Engines

While most people will make regular use of search engines, only a few might know about how to refine a search in order to make it most effective. As Google is the most popular search engine at the time of writing, we will focus on its specific functions. Many of the aspects enumerated in table 5.3 are true for other search engines as well however.

Number of words	The fewer words you use, the more search results you will get an increase in the number of search words will narrow down the number of search results	Funtions of search engines
Types of words	There is no need for capital letters, prepositions or articles as most search engines ignore them	
Refining searches	What you are looking for should be in the first 30-50 results – if it isn't you should possibly think of new search words	
Local versions	For finding country specific information use the local sites of search engine, e.g. google.co.uk for Great Britain	

The + symbol	The + sign in front of a word indicates that a word must be on the displayed web page
The – symbol	The – sign in front of a word indicates that no site with the indicated word should be included
Or	Inserting an "or" between two words indicates that pages have to include either one or both of these two words
Double quotation marks ".."	If you type in an expression using double quotation marks, the exact expression will be looked for on the pages
The ~	The ~ in front of a word will result in Google searching for pages with this word or synonyms of the word
Searching one site	You can limit the search to one site with the words or expression, followed by site: URL of the site, e.g. "human rights" site:www.bbc.co.uk; this kind of search might be particularly useful for sites which don't have a search function
Searching online glossaries	If you want to find a definition of a word or expression, you can type in definition: followed by the entry, e.g. definition: lexicography. Google will then search online glossaries
Google News	Google News will only search in results on news pages, e.g. newspapers, TV channels or news magazines .
Asterisk *	*The asterisk * character can be used as a filler, e.g. if one types in "we would like to * information", one might find entries, such as "we would like to find information" or "we would like to gather information"*

Table 5.3: Search functions of search engines (adapted from Sharma & Barrett 2007: 16ff.; contents in italics added)

Using search engines in class

The information people look for differs greatly as do the options for finding information (see table 5.3 above). To google includes the options of finding out about something or someone by typing in the search word in question into Google. Also, now the variety of situations in which people choose to google something increases tremendously as smartphones make it possible to search the web almost everywhere. In English lessons search engines can fulfil various functions. They can be used for finding information on basically everything, e.g. on language issues as well as on famous people, regions, events or current affairs. Task based, inquiry based or project based learning environments will provide an authentic environment for using search engines. Typical related activities are comparing information found online, searching for content presented in different kinds of media or genres, finding and evaluating opposing arguments from different sources. Also, internet research is often used as a preparation for creative work (see chapters 4.6, 5.6).

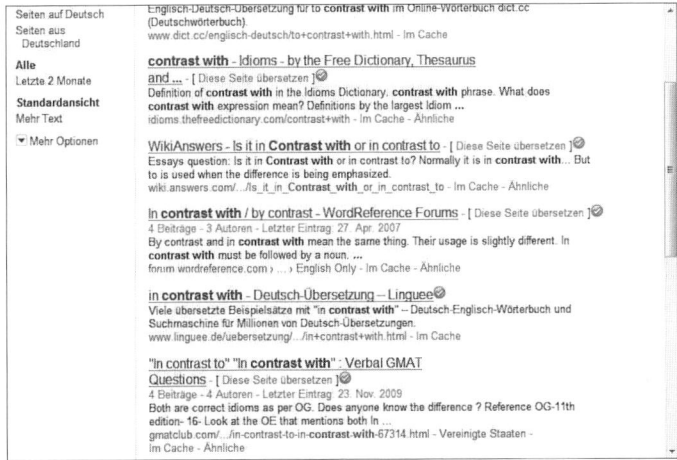

Screenshot 5.6: The use of Google as a concordancer

Search engines are generally used as reference tools for multiple functions and can certainly be employed with their multiple functions during task or project based work. Thus, in addition to the function of gaining and checking information Google is also used for editing texts, e.g. for checking the accuracy and style of a text. This is often done by typing in a particular expression into the search engine in "." (see table 5.3) in order to see the number of hits and the contexts the expression is used in. In this function Google has also been called "a quick'n dirty concordancer" (Chinnery 2008, Robb 2003) as it quickly gives you an idea of whether the used collocation is right or whether the spelling you used is the correct one. For more ideas on how to use search engines for the purpose of composing and editing texts see table 5.3.

The quality of search results
A quality check of the hits found is quite important here as some frequent misspellings and errors in language use can often be found on the web, especially as not all sites are published by native speakers of English. In this context it would be interesting to type in alternative options and to see how well-accepted the sites listed by Google in our search results are. The dict.cc site that appears quite high up in the ranks of the search results above (see screenshot 5.6), for example, is a well-established which can be regarded as fairly credible.

In connection with the use of search engines the ability to evaluate materials quickly and effectively is extremely important if the students are not to get lost in the wealth of information. The students incidentally practise their skimming and scanning skills while working on meaningful tasks using search engines. Students should still be made aware of useful strategies and techniques for effective internet research, e.g. including the information given in table 5.3.

RSS Feeds and Personal Virtual Environments

Delivery of information
New developments in programming and software development mean that we do not necessarily have to actively look out for information on topics that we are interested in any more. The subscription to RSS (Real Simple Syndication) feeds means that we get an e-mail with updates on news which is published on a particular site in general or on specific chosen issues as soon as they are published. That means that news does not have to be actively found on the web but is delivered to us.

There are also more and more programmes that allow users to create a personalized virtual environment (see Godwin-Jones 2009) in which news from different sites is put together in a clear structure. iGoogle offers such an option, for example, and another of those programmes is Pageflake (see screenshot 5.7; pageflakes.com). Pageflakes has got options, such as including one's teaching schedule into VLE which certainly makes it interesting for teachers. The news on the personalized site is updated frequently, so that someone who has chosen to always stay informed on what is going on on *Facebook*, *Twitter* and *Yourtube*, about the weather and news from a chosen Online magazine, does not need to visit the individual sites in order to stay up to date but just needs to look at the corner of the screen that has been chosen for this type of news. Personalized virtual environments can only play a role in English lessons where students are allowed to make choices and to work autonomously to some extent.

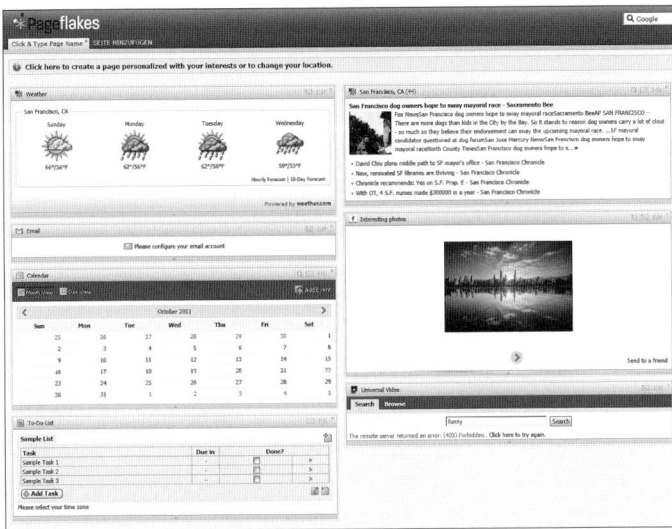

Screenshot 5.7: A screenshot of the starter page of Pageflake

Social Bookmarking Sites

Guidance for the wealth of information on the net is also provided by social bookmarking services such as delicious or digg. Here each user can publish his or her selected bookmarks. On digg everyone can publish a link to interesting materials they find. Others rate this link and the published comments by either *digging* it, which is positive, or, if they do not like it, by *burying* it.

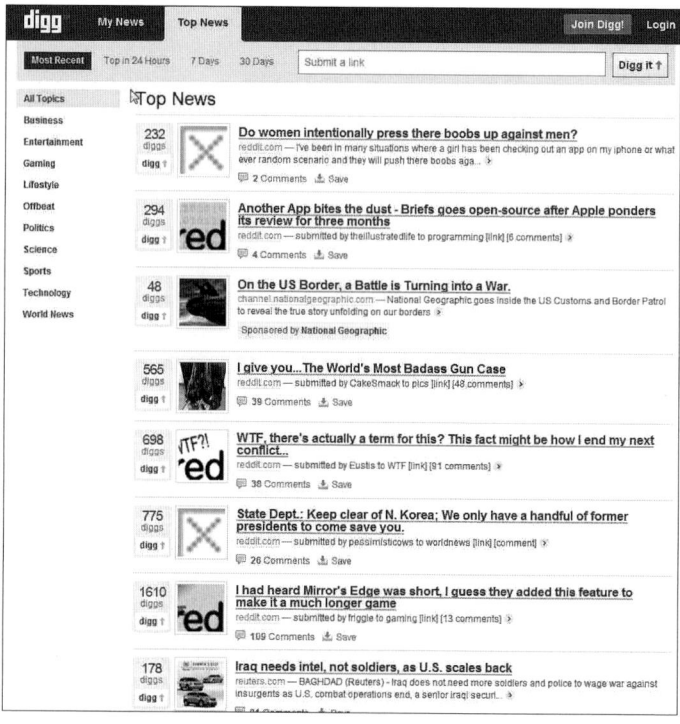

Screenshot 5.8: Top News suggestions on the digg site

Viewing rated
information

Screenshot 5.8 shows that there is a big variety of topics and different types of comments here. People might consult those sites in a casual manner but most people will either take a liking to the type of information provided as well as the type of interaction or, if not, will soon stop consulting a particular social bookmarking site. For use in schools this application can be helpful if students want to inform themselves on the latest news in a particular field of interest, e.g. entertainment or sports. Also, the published comments are authentic accounts of target language use as well as an insight into how specific issues are rated by large numbers of people. As bookmarking sites are social in nature and allow the active communities to upload their links and views with ease, the services fall under the category of social software which will be discussed in more detail in chapter 8.

Surfing the net safely

One reason why teachers might prefer WebQuests and other, more guided activities on the web to using search engines in lessons is net safety. Asking students to do interesting and topic related research for articles and pictures on the www does bear some risks. Anyone who has typed in a supposedly harmless word such as "banana" into a search engine in order to find a picture of the fruit might have experienced some dubious links coming up together with those one was looking for. Some careful thinking has to be done before one defines the search expressions (see above) and the more open the students' research, the bigger the danger that they might come into contact with inappropriate material even without intending to. Most search engines do have an adult contents filter that filters out pornographic sites for example. For Google the instructions for activating such a filter can be found under settings. The filters are not perfect though – apparently not all inappropriate sites are identified while some harmless contents are blocked.

With the knowledge that there is no way of making free use of the world wide web at school 100% safe, those in education may come to different conclusions: They may decide not to use the web at all which would be a shame as they would lose the chance to get hold of authentic materials and it would also be questionable from an educational point of view. If schools are to guide students through their youth and prepare them for their future lives, then lessons at school cannot ignore the fact that students do spend a lot of their time on the web and that web literacy for students' future jobs and their lives in general is important. Some educators and researchers suggest tackling the legal problems that arise from exposing students to the danger of the web by involving students and parents in discussions and decisions about net safety rather than fighting a losing battle by trying to keep them 100% safe from accessing inappropriate material (Müller-Hartmann & Raith 2009, Richardson 2009). In this way students learn to deal with these contents in a responsible way and develop media literacy that can save them from greater harm.

For those who decide that they don't want to take these risks, there is a whole range of safe search engines for younger students that employ humans in order to block pages with contents

Responsible use of the web

that should not be viewed by children and teenagers. The site SearchEngineWatch.com offers a comprehensive list of links and good information on the most common search engines for kids. Some of the better known search engines for kids are listed in table 5.4.

Search Engine	URL
Ask for Kids	http://www.askkids.com/
KidsClick!	http://www.kidsclick.org/
Yahoo Kids	http://kids.yahoo.com/
Fact Monster	http//www.factmonster.com/

Table 5.4: A Collection of Kids search engines

5.4 Focus on Research

How good are the WebQuests on the web and how well do they support learning?

On the success of WebQuests

A lot has been said about WebQuests but most of the published documents are somewhat descriptive, focusing on either the general qualities of WebQuests, giving criteria for choosing or designing good WebQuests or providing samples of good practice. This is one of the conclusions of Abbit's and Ophus's 2008 review of the research that has been done on WebQuests. They agree with Milson's judgement who stated in 2002 that most of the publications on WebQuests were "anecdotal accounts of success" (Milson 2002: 335). Being afraid that WebQuests might be hyped and used in schools because they seem to be promising but that real learning outcomes might lag behind expectation levels (also see Maddux & Cummings 2007), Abbit and Ophus set out to see how many and what kinds of real research results there really are that support these anecdotal stories. They found that the results were very mixed.

A lot of the research that has been done focused on students' attitudes. The main findings were that students seemed to prefer

WebQuests to textbook based activities but were inclined to stop when an activity seemed difficult (Murray 2006) and reported a wear off effect within the two week period covered by the WebQuest in the study.

Abbit and Ophus also found that most studies supported the assumption that WebQuests facilitate and require collaboration among students. While students did find the collaboration challenging at times (Leahy and Twomey 2005), most students regarded the collaboration as beneficial (Kortecamp and Bartoshesky 2003; Leahy and Twomey 2005).

Research on the impact of WebQuests on students' learning and their level of achievement found mostly that there was no advantage in using WebQuests compared to more traditional methods. Most research focusing on these aspects was carried out using control groups, with both groups sitting the same kinds of exams in the end. Here we do have to say that we know too little about the different studies in order to be able to judge their validity. It is, for example, worth considering that the exams have to mirror the learning that has taken place beforehand. If the WebQuests were project based and focused on skills development, strategies of collaboration and problem solving, a test with formats that mostly test students' knowledge and accuracy will not be appropriate in order to assess what has really been learned.

Abbit and Ophus also report on studies related to the cognitive requirements of WebQuests. They describe findings by Kanuka, Rourke, and Laflamme (2007) who claim that WebQuests are more effective at creating a higher cognitive presence than some other activities. Other researchers, e.g. Molebash, Dodge, Bell, and Mason (2002) however, claim that it might be difficult to support higher order thinking skills through Webquests as they found that the majority of WebQuests, they could find online, required structured inquiries, some fostered guided inquiry and none of the WebQuests they looked at supported open inquiries that could, from their point of view, lead to real higher order thinking.

Concluding from the research Abbit and Ophus report on, we can summarize that some researchers do not find that WebQuests are effective at supporting learning in the traditional sense, while others claim that they are not open enough for real learning. While this meta-research gives us a good overview of what has been said about WebQuests so far, it also makes clear that, when talking about WebQuests, we have to make sure that we talk about the same kind of activity, as some researchers are very restricitive about what they regard as a WebQuest, while others would more or less call anything that uses web-based formats a WebQuest. Also, when testing outcomes, we might need research that uses methods for testing the outcomes of WebQuests that match the learning that takes place during a WebQuest. For this kind of research it is also important to know, where the biggest potentials of WebQuests lie, i.e. what we would like to achieve and what we can and cannot achieve with the help of this kind of learning.

5.5 Classroom Ideas

What kind of WebQuest could inspire higher order thinking?

The idea of WebQuests as a good introduction to internet research as well as an efficient framework for structured projects on a chosen topic has already been discussed earlier in this chapter. The sample WebQuest presented focused on planning a trip to Australia. This is a tourist kit approach (Grimm 2010) that will motivate students as Australia is quite a popular destination for tourists. If students are really to learn more about the country, however, they should at some stage get below this surface. Focusing on the so-called "stolen generation" is one option of dealing with Australia's history and the attitude towards the Aboriginal culture. There is a good book and an accompanying film, called "Rabbit-proof fence" (Pilkington Garimara 1996) that can serve as a good introduction to the topic. There is also the option of creating a WebQuest on the topic or using an existing one, such as the one created in Tobias Unger's class at the University of Marburg.

Screenshot 5.9: A WebQuest on the Stolen Generation (taken from: http://sgwebquest.wordpress.com/)

The aim of the chosen WebQuest is to create a newspaper article on the Stolen Generation in a small group, with general information being given and links to sites on specific aspects being provided within the WebQuest. The leading question is whether it is enough if the Australian government apologizes for what they have done to the Aboriginal people of Australia or whether other measures would be necessary.

While we would rather suggest that each group should work on a different kind of article, focusing on different aspects, we do think that this kind of WebQuest can trigger higher order thinking and creativity.

Tasks

1. Think about your strategies for searching the web. Note down
   - The sites/applications that you refer to most often
   - Your criteria for judging a site
   - The purposes for which you use search engines.
2. In a group of four, work on the WebQuest about WebQuests that Dodge has created (see table 5.1). Be prepared to present your judgements on the best WebQuest in your class.

3. Within your groups, now look at one of the WebQuests from March's *Best WebQuests* site. Look for one that is real, rich and relevant from all your points of view.
4. In your group, come up with at least one good idea for a WebQuest (topic, outcomes & rough procedures).
5. Discuss the general potential for WebQuests in English lessons. Where do you see the advantages and where do you see the limitations? Take notes of your results in this or a similar way:

Potentials	Limitations
Aspects we could not agree on:	

6. Referring to your results from tasks 1-5, create a list of conditions that need to be fulfilled if you want to make full use of the potential WebQuests have for English lessons.
7. Choose a search word/expression and type it into at least three different search engines. Note down any differences that you can observe and pros or cons that you see.
8. List at least three different types of uses of Google in English lessons. Refer to the information given in the chapter and come up with concrete classroom ideas.
9. Check out one bookmarking site and try to find information that you are interested in. Then discuss in a group whether you would be motivated to become an active member of the community. Give reasons for your decision.
10. Within your group, share your prior experience with using personalized virtual environments. If possible, show each other the sites that you use and discuss the benefits and downsides of different offers plus the concept of personalizing virtual environments.

TOOLS FOR TEACHERS | 6

6.1 Overview

Is it realistically possible to teach a foreign language today without any assistance from digital media?

In this chapter we are investigating the use of computers for language teaching explicitly from the teacher's perspective. Computers do not only play a role as learning tools in the classroom, but they also influence language teaching through the work teachers do at their desks at home. Having said this, a clear-cut distinction between home and classroom use isn't easy. For example, teachers use web resources as a preparation for lessons as well as in the classroom itself later on, or they use an electronic tool to produce a worksheet which is then used by the learners.

For the purposes of this book we have decided to draw the reader's attention to four such "tools" which deserve specific attention because of their potential for developing language teaching, and which cannot easily be subsumed under the other chapter headings.

To begin with, there are a range of authoring tools which enable teachers to design their own electronic materials (6.2). Another more specific type of software, "diagnostic tools", which are meant to diagnose the learners' level of competence, are only beginning to emerge but clearly hold promise for the field of differentiated and individualized teaching (6.3).So-called learning management systems like Moodle or Blackboard which offer a broader E-learning environment for (language) classrooms are also in a way teacher tools even though they are also implemented later on in classroom work (6.4). Finally, we have decided to put Interactive Whiteboards in this chapter even though they are hardware (but to be used with specific software, 6.5). As in the other chapters, final attention will be given to research and classroom ideas in the field of teacher tools.

6.2 Authoring software

How much time do teachers have besides their teaching to develop their own (electronic) materials?

As the name suggests, authoring tools allow the user to 'author' his or her own materials rather than taking over ready-made samples. Typically, teachers might want to develop their own exercises because they are not satisfied with the available tasks (e.g. from coursebooks), or because they feel the need to customize materials to meet the needs of individual learners. To some extent teachers have always composed their own teaching and learning items, but possibilities have certainly been enhanced through digital media. There are a number of software packages that allow the easy creation of paper-based exercises. Even though it is arguable whether such packages are authoring software in a stricter sense (since the outcome is non-digital), we would like to include them here because they are typical tools for teachers and can have quite some influence on the teaching process. An example of such a product is Lingofox which converts texts into

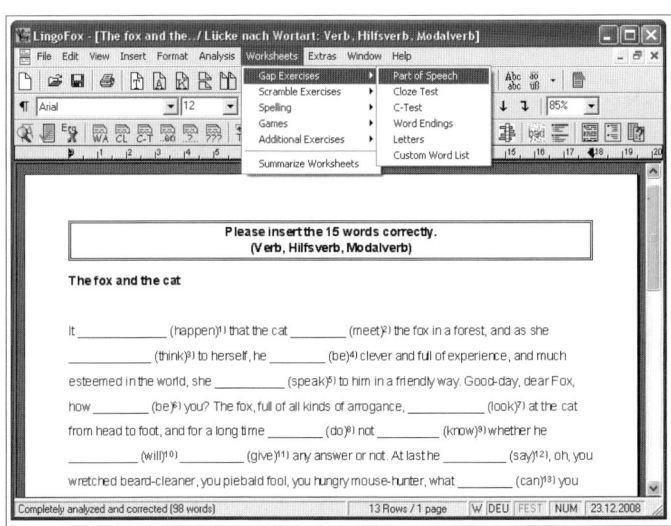

Screenshot 6.1: Automatic creation of a verb-based exercise in Lingofox

various exercise formats (e.g. scramble exercises, matching, cloze). If these tools are equipped with some kind of database with the underlying target language (as is the case with Lingofox) it is possible to create some 'semi-intelligent' exercises like the one in the screenshot where all the verbs of a text are removed automatically and provided in brackets.

A simple tool for designing puzzles can be found online under puzzlemaker.com. With this tool you can easily create crossword puzzles, word search puzzles and many more formats that can be copied and pasted into your word processor and printed.

Easy creation of interactive activities

Besides such tools producing a paper-based outcome, authoring software typically refers to tools which allow the user to develop interactive materials. With regard to complexity, such packages range from very elaborate products (e.g. Adobe Authorware) which already resemble programming languages, to more undemanding tools which can be managed after a short training period. An example of the latter is a free web-based package called 'Hot Potatoes' which lets the user construct various exercise formats (e.g. matching, gap filling, crossword). After providing the necessary data, the result is then displayed as an interactive web page which can be distributed online, via a school server or any other medium (Hot Potatoes exercises can also be embedded into Learning management systems, see 6.4).

The following screenshot shows the authoring environment of the matching tool in Hot Potatoes.

Screenshot 6.2: Creating a matching activity with Hot Potatoes

Another example of an easy-to-use authoring tool is a software series called 'The Authoring Suite' which comprises a number of different formats. Among these, the 'Storyboard' idea has gained some eminence in the CALL community. The basic idea is that a text is converted into a series of blobs where each blob stands for a letter. The learner hast to reconstruct the original text in as few attempts as possible.

Using Storyboard for language teaching

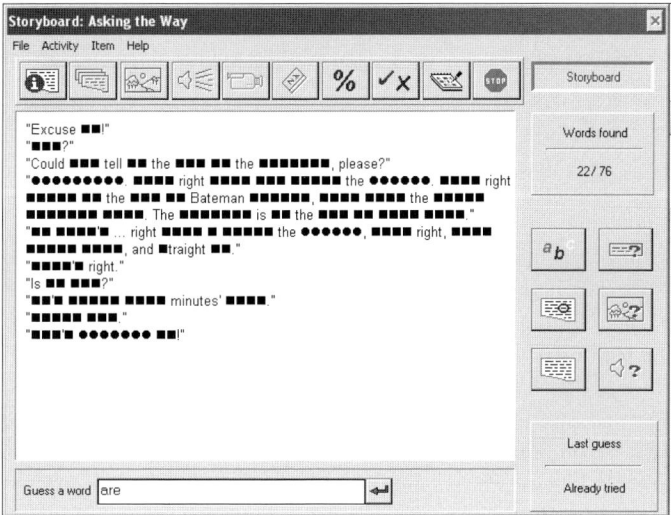

Screenshot 6.3: 'Storyboard' – replacing text by blobs

There are now also many tools online to help create materials easily. A free tool for creating quizzes is Fling the Teacher (see screenshot 6.4) created by Content Generator (contentgenerator.net). After having customized their teacher, the students' incentive for answering all the 15 questions correctly is to be able to build a trebuchet and fling the teacher. It is as easy to create as a paper version and is a fun way of checking students' knowledge.

Fling the teacher

Regardless of the exact type of authoring software, the question asked at the outset of this sub-chapter remains significant: to what extent can teachers create their own materials, and is it realistic to presume that teachers automatically have all the necessary expertise it needs to produce first-class teaching materials, furthermore in the field of interactive digital media?

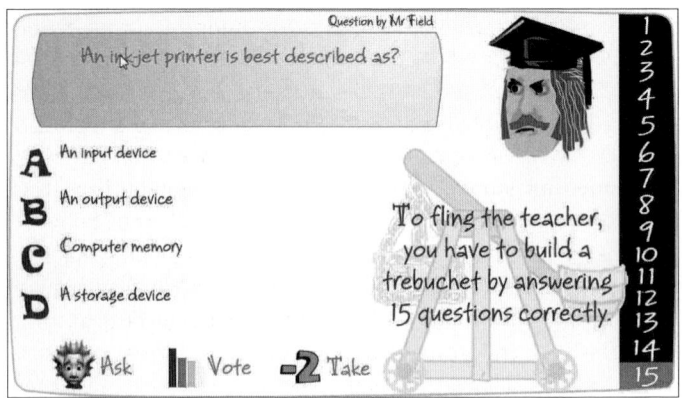

Screenshot 6.4: An example site of a "Fling the teacher" quiz (taken from: http://www.contentgenerator.net/fling/)

A second issue, which is just as crucial, regards the way the products belonging to such authoring tools are integrated into the teaching process. One interesting approach might be to involve the learners in the authoring process too, i.e. turning students into authors of digital media. This proposal will be taken up later on (see 6.7), after the discussion of some further teacher tools.

6.3 Diagnostic tools

What kinds of tools did your teachers use for diagnosis in English lessons? What other tools do you know?

Diagnosis, generally defined as "investigation or analysis of a cause or nature of a condition, situation or problem" (Merriam Webster 2010), has become a bit of a buzz word in German educational contexts over the last couple of years. Part of the reason might have to do with the dissatisfaction with the PISA results German students got in the past and the educational consequences that have been discussed since. While most educators would agree that students should be involved as much as possible in the process of diagnosis and assessment as well as in the decision making processes in order to support autonomy and lifelong learning, a lot of practitioners still see diagnosis as something that has to be done to the students by experts in order to ensure that they get the best possible feedback and support.

The tools for diagnosis range from portfolios that have been developed for students' self-assessment to standardized tests that are supposed to give an insight into a student's abilities or preferences. In Anglophone contexts one also distinguishes between summative and formative assessment. While summative assessment is product oriented and gives students a clear, quantifiable statement on how good a product is, formative assessment focuses on how to actually support students in the process of learning and would rather be done through written or oral comments, goal setting on the side of the students and joint reflections. Summative and formative assessment

Standardized tests for the diagnosis of language skills which belong to the category of summative assessment or, in other words, result oriented diagnosis, have always had their place in education, for example for students who wished to study abroad. With ongoing globalization, a move towards implementing more standardized exams in schools and the endeavour by Germany to shorten the time before the *Abitur* to 8 years, the pressure for teachers and learners to constantly monitor their progress has grown immensely. The wealth of study materials and tests that are developed and used for diagnosing student's language levels and for supporting their progress, shows that there is a visible tendency towards drilling students to pass the centralized exams. While this is an understandable short-term reaction towards looming exams, we do hope that this will not lead to a culture of just teaching for the test in lessons.

Tests on paper have to be graded by the teacher and even if they are standardized, this still means work that in many cases can be done by a machine. Standardized online tests that assess students' language levels have a long tradition in the university sector. There are adaptive tests that react to how successful students are in certain areas in order to fine-tune the results. Most tests are simply online versions of the straightforward offline tests however. Standardized tests

Textbook publishers have started to develop this kind of standardized tests for different year groups and subjects at Online tests school. The site fördern@cornelsen.de, for example, provides tests and subsequent exercises for students of registered and paying teachers or schools. The exercises and tasks that are suggested to students after having done the test are differentiated with regard to the students' level of English in listening comprehension, reading comprehension and a so-called general language ability.

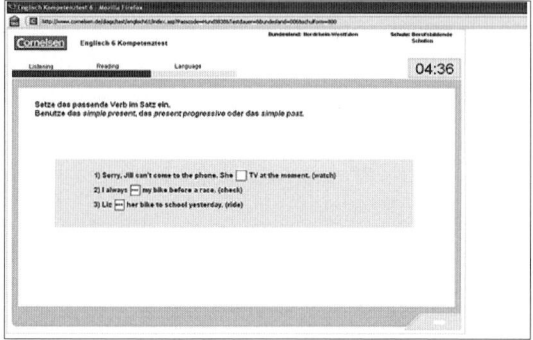

Screenshot 6.5: A sample exercise from the Cornelsen Fördern online diagnosis test

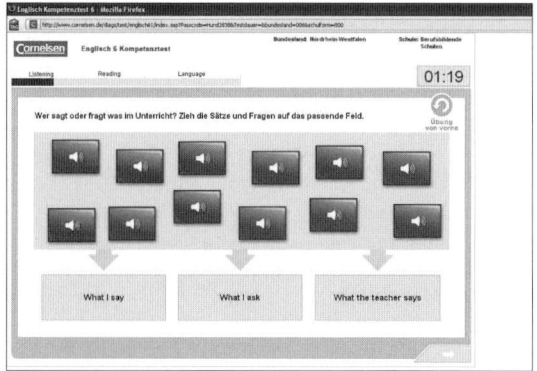

Screenshot 6.6: A sample listening task from the Cornelsen Fördern online diagnosis test

In screenshot 6.5 you can see a grammar exercise from the test for year 6. The time for the exercises and tasks are limited. In the top right corner you can see the timer that can be seen by the students while they are working. Screenshot 6.6 shows a matching task that tests the listening skills of students.

One advantage of those tests is that they also include the skills of listening and reading comprehension instead of just focusing on grammar, vocabulary and writing. The disadvantages are that they are static, i.e. not adapting to the students' or classes' level of English and that the validity of the tests is not clear. In table 6.1 you find the summarized feedback of a student group from a course run by Meike Strohn at the University of Bochum after having evaluated a year 6 test and the study materials.

	positive aspects:	negative aspects:
method/ form/ design:	• less effort for diagnosing process and evaluation than manual tests • clear design and easy to use • quick test and immediate evaluation (quick results) • possibility to listen twice to every item • possibility to restart the exercise • "Lernbereichsanzeiger" → students always know where they are (middle, reading etc.), provides orientation • clear structure • proposed "Förderpläne" → support for teachers • individual results as well as comparative results to class can be shown → teacher can either see where one student has problems or where the main problems of the class are	• very standardized test (although this is also positive in the sense that it makes the results reliable), may be under or above the average class level • clock running in the background only leads to anxiety (although it might be good to check how long it takes the students to finish) • if you make a mistake, you have to restart the whole exercise • mainly receptive skills are tested; although there is a gap-fill exercise for diagnosing strengths & weaknesses in the field of tenses • items in wrong order or sequence concerning the listening activities → confusion • quality of the "Förderpläne" is questionable • the teacher only gets the results for each language area, but cannot see the respective mistakes the student made

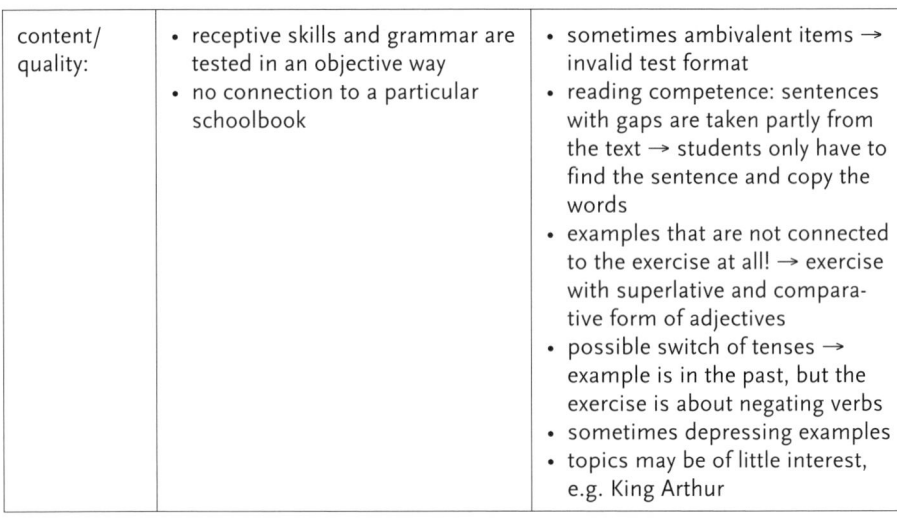

| content/ quality: | • receptive skills and grammar are tested in an objective way
• no connection to a particular schoolbook | • sometimes ambivalent items → invalid test format
• reading competence: sentences with gaps are taken partly from the text → students only have to find the sentence and copy the words
• examples that are not connected to the exercise at all! → exercise with superlative and comparative form of adjectives
• possible switch of tenses → example is in the past, but the exercise is about negating verbs
• sometimes depressing examples
• topics may be of little interest, e.g. King Arthur |

Table 6.1: Feedback on the Cornelsen Fördern online diagnosis test

A free online test for assessing students' or your own level in reading, writing, listening and knowledge of grammar and vocabulary in English is, at the time of writing, provided by the University of Lancaster. The battery of tests for 14 different languages is called Dialang (http://www.lancs.ac.uk/researchenterprise/dialang/about<). The tests, developed by different European Universities, are static, i.e. they are not adaptive and, at the time of writing, they have not been developed further as the funding has ceased. There are three levels that users can choose themselves. The tests have been developed with regard to the Common European Framework of Reference (CEFR) and do thus refer to standards that have been agreed on internationally. But again, it is not clear from the information given how valid the test is and how much it really says about a learner's language proficiency.

Using portfolios for ongoing assessment

Educators, who argue in favour of portfolios as a tool for ongoing reflections, would claim that a look at a portfolio gives a more holistic and valuable insight into a student's progress, abilities and interests than just considering test the results of a standardized test. Also, portfolio work does not necessarily exclude the use of standardized tests. The results of those tests can be included in one part of the portfolio, as well as the results of questionnaires concerning interests, learning styles and accounts of students' ongoing self-assessment. There is usually also a section in which students show their abilities and their creativity by displaying work they have done and projects they have been part of. There is no doubt that this is a more complete and individualized way of monitoring and supporting students – the "downsides" are that getting and keeping an overview of the students' progress and the ongoing joint reflections do take time. Teachers might find it difficult to integrate them into their tight curriculum. Also, if used as a means for applications, a hardcopy portfolio is not as easy to copy and send away as an exam certificate or a report.

E-portfolios can be seen as a solution to this, however, as just the link to the portfolio site or the digital files have to be sent.

While portfolios were in the past mostly used in fields in which some kind of artistic or at least creative work was done, in order to give an overview of former achievements and personal styles, exhibiting a kind of personal profile, for example through social networks like Xing, is common practice for almost everyone who is working on his or her career nowadays. Also, personal websites or blogs are now replacing the old-fashioned printed portfolio in most professions. So, working with portfolios does reflect the developments outside of school.

The option of creating e-portfolios is now, for example, part of all Learning Management Systems in one way or the other, be it in the form of a blog or wiki or in form of a fully blown framework for a portfolio. Other, open-source software products that can be used for creating e-portfolios are, at the time of writing, mahara.org (see screenshot 6.7) or elgg.org. As in the case of other social software products, special care has to be given to the current terms and conditions in order to assure that the users' privacy is secured and that the rights for the published materials are clear.

Portfolios can take many forms. They can focus either mostly on the development of a student, or they can be put together for the purpose of presentation, just like the portfolios of artists, or alternatively they can be combined portfolios that are used for assessment and feedback from a tutor or mentor. For more information on what portfolios can consist of or on how to create an e-portfolio consult any of the sites listed in table 6.2.

(margin note) e-portfolios

(margin note) Information on (e-) portfolios

Screenshot 6.7: The intro page of the Mahara.org online portfolio site

e-teaching.org/ lehrszenarien/ pruefung/ pruefungsform/ eportfolio/	E-teaching.org is a non-commercial portal that provides general information on how to design learning environments using New Media. The section on e-portfolios provides a first overview of the functions of an e-portfolio in a range of other options for assessment.
e-portfolios.org/	This site that has been put together by an individual person, Hartmut Haefele, provides good information on different programmes that can be used for creating e-portfolios, their pros and cons.
e-portfolio.at/	The site, run by the e-portfolio initiative Austria, is mostly describing an initiative that has been started in Austria. It can be helpful for teachers in schools to see how the initiative is working, what their aims are and how teachers can implement e-portfolios into their assessment procedures themselves.

Table 6.2: A short collection of informative sites on online portfolios

6.4 Learning Management Systems

Have you ever worked with Moodle, ILIAS or Blackboard? What is your attitude to these Learning Management Systems?

Learning Management Systems (LMS), also referred to as Virtual Learning Environments (VLE), provide a secured environment for any kind of online work. They have been popular for organizing university courses for years, so you might have used one of the major Learning Management Systems, such as Moodle, ILIAS or Blackboard yourself already. All LMS provide the option of setting up password secured courses, a feature that makes them attractive for use within institutions, i.e. if no completely open exchange of information is wanted.

This feature is also particularly interesting for schools as it makes it possible to combine the use of authentic resources and many different applications with a structured and relatively safe learning environment.

Important features of LMS

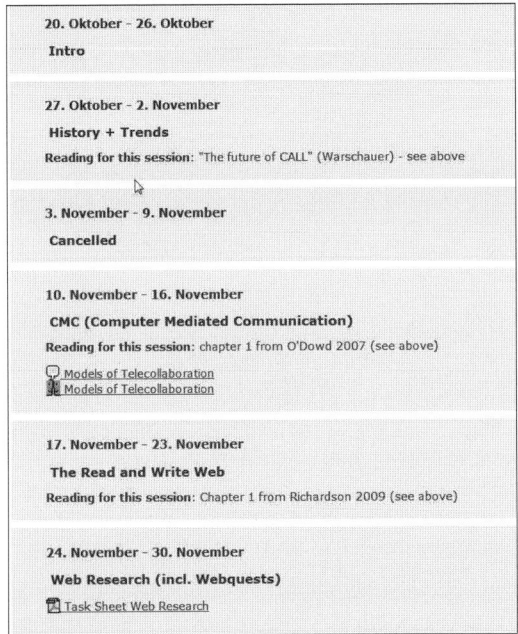

Screenshot 6.8: One possible course structure within Moodle

For the organization of a course this means that all resources, such as worksheets, texts or links to websites, can be provided online. Also, tasks and contents for each session can be published. In screenshot 6.8 you can see a chronological organization of a Moodle course with entries for each session, whereas in screenshot 6.9 the organization is topic related.

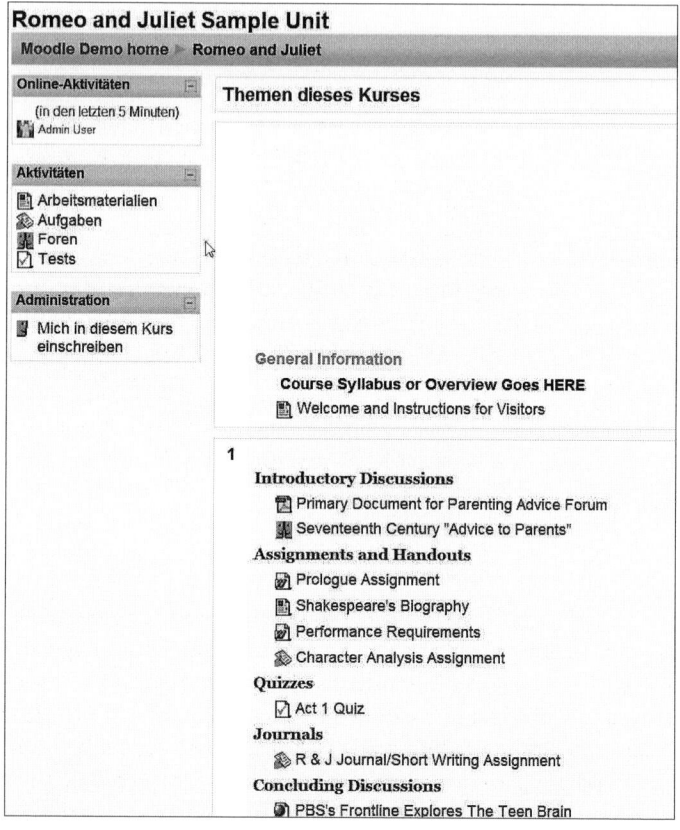

Screenshot 6.9: A content based organization of contents within Moodle (taken from: http://demo.moodle.net/course/view.php?id=596)

Choice of LMS   As Moodle is the biggest LMS with the greatest number of users and also is an open-source product, which means that using the software package is for free, most of our descriptions are about Moodle features – a lot of those features are shared by other well known LMSs which are briefly described in table 6.3 however.

Apart from those more established learning management systems there are many more open-source software products emerging that may or may not gain recognition. Among those tools are Claroline (claroline.net) which has been developed for educational purposes and Chamilo (campus.chamilo.org) which was launched in 2010.

ILIAS	ILIAS is another popular virtual learning environment that can be run on an open-source basis and is, for example, used by some universities in Germany. It offers the opportunity of creating whole online modules for learning. Each user has his or her own desktop with courses they have registered for, RSS feeds, personal notes, a personal schedule and more. The options for course structures are similar to the Moodle structures, as are the options for activities.
Blackboard	Blackboard is a web based commercial educational software product for designing e-campi. The software consists of several modules that allow teachers to create online learning modules, post announcements, due dates or assignments, to communicate with their students. The activities and features are similar to those of Moodle and ILIas. Blackboard has been widely used in the Anglophone world and has also been implemented by some universities in Germany. The software has been criticised for being expensive to run however.

Table 6.3: A brief overview of the features of the Content Management Systems ILIAS & Blackboard

Functions of Moodle

One really useful function of Learning Management systems, such as Moodle, is that students, once they are registered for a course, are listed under the section participants. The teacher can then send e-mails to individual or all students by selecting them from a list which often includes the name, a photo, if the student has uploaded one, and information about when the student last entered the online system. In this way the list of participants even includes a control function, provided it is activated in your setting.

Apart from the option of sending e-mails to each other, there are the forum and the chat as main communication tools. In the forum, which is an asynchronous communication tool (see chapter 3.3), important issues can be discussed, experiences exchanged or questions asked. Chats, being synchronous communication tools (see chapter 3.2), require that everyone who wants to take part in the communication has to be logged on at the same time. This makes most sense for distant learning courses and not necessarily for lessons in which students are all present although it might be a good opportunity for those students who are more self confident in writing rather than speaking in English, to take part in a classroom discussion. A chat can also be helpful when experts who are not present in the room are interviewed or when partner classes are involved in the discussion. The good thing about integrating forum discussions and chats into Moodle is that the communication takes place within a secured environment, i.e. students are not subject to the same dangers as in open chat rooms and forums.

The same is true for the blogs (for more information see chapter 8.4) received automatically by each Moodle user. One can decide whether one just wants to use the blog as a private journal, whether it should be viewable within the closed group, so that others can see and evaluate one's work or whether it should be open to the general public. Blogs can be used for creative work, they can link to each other and, as often happens in school projects, they can be linked to the main website of the school and can serve as a site that demonstrates the results of a project.

Screenshot 6.10: Important features of Moodle (taken from: http://moodle.uni-duisburg-essen.de/course/view.php?id=2350)

There are many different activities and resources a teacher can create or upload. Activities that can be added to the grids are, for example, forum discussions or chats with the option of timing activities and grouping students. There is also the opportunity of adding a wiki (see chapter 8.3 for more information), surveys, glossaries the students create or questionnaires, e.g. for the evaluation of courses.

While Moodle courses are still more text based and often look less attractive than, e.g. a blog in which pictures and other links can be integrated more easily, there are certainly a lot of options for enriching English classes through the use of such a Learning Management System. Also, LMS in general are now, at the time of writing, getting more flexible when it comes to integrating applications from outside the system. This makes them less static and more flexible when it comes to integrating creative work, e.g. quizzes, such as the Hot Potatoes quiz that has been created in Moodle by Stefanie Welzel for the use in the primary classroom.

Integrating web 2.0 tools into LMS

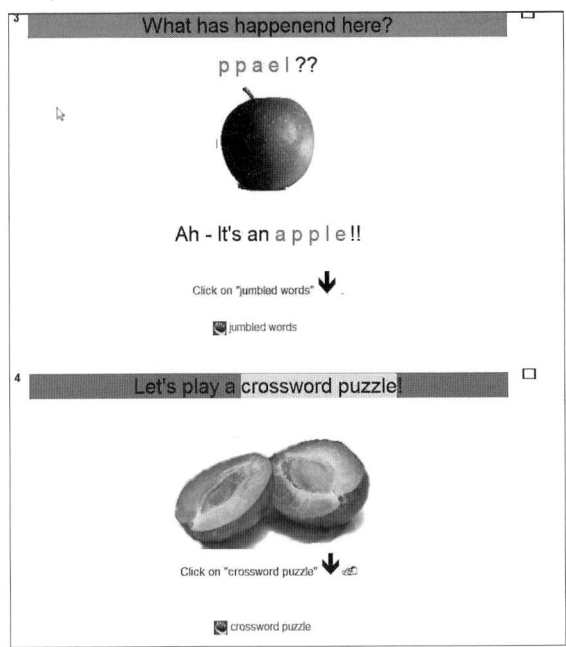

Screenshot 6.11: A Hot Potatoes Quiz within Moodle (Taken from: http://www.moodleschule.de/course/view.php?id=685&edit=0&ses skey=LgMvRbPyvO)

The community of Moodle users is big and active. On sites, such as *moodle.org, moodleschule.de* and *moodle.de* you will find a lot of information on Moodle itself, on how to use it and also on the big Moodle community that organizes international Moodle conferences, the so-called Moodle-Moots.

From the presentations of schools and workshops at these Moots you can get the impression that Moodle is, within the community, used in many different ways. The platform is used to organize whole projects, such as the Romeo and Juliet project in snapshot 6.9, it is used as a platform for e-portfolios and peer assessment but it is also used for the organization of traditional classroom work and for exam preparation. Their high level of versatility is one of the big advantages of Learning Management Systems – they do not necessitate a certain type of methodology in order to be of real help for learners and teachers.

6.5 Interactive Whiteboards

How do you think the use of Interactive Whiteboard has an impact on English lessons?

Although interactive whiteboards are hardware, they are included here as the specific software that goes along with them accounts for a lot of their characteristics. Abroad, e.g. in the UK, you will find interactive whiteboards in many classrooms, from the primary up to the tertiary level. In Germany, at the time of writing, there is one in many secondary schools and there are many in the tertiary sector but at primary level you find only very few interactive whiteboards, at the moment mostly in private schools. We hope that this will change as primary school students could profit at least as much from the many options that interactive whiteboards offer as older learners.

Overview of basic features
In its simplest form it could be seen as a big screen for projecting of anything one would want to project in class, be it films, websites or traditional worksheets. The hardware is normally ordered with a sound system, so any sound in combination with visual stimuli can be displayed, be it written or a set of pictures.

That means that there are many new options for making class-room work more multimodal and multifaceted.

One of the major features of interactive whiteboards is that they have huge touch screens that can either be touched with the hands or with specific pens. Within the interactive whiteboard software and in many games, items on the screen can be moved around, so especially kinaesthetic drag and drop matching or ordering tasks can be done together in class. Also, quizzes like the Moodle ones shown in screenshot 6.11 can be joint class activities.

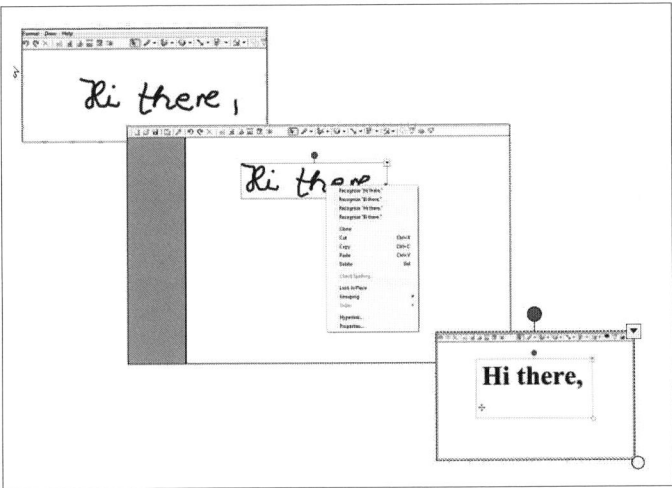

Screenshot 6.12: The text recognition tool of the Smartboard software

The interactive whiteboard software has so many functions of that it will not be possible to enumerate them all here. One of the big advantages for the work with all ages is that the writing that has been done within a lesson can be saved. It can even be turned into typed script if the writing is reasonably legible. In screenshot 6.12 you can see the process of writing, right clicking and choosing from the options provided and then the typed script.

In screenshot 6.13 it shows a very simple sample file created with Smartboard software which is one of the major brands of interactive whiteboards at the moment. You can see that it can be really easy to create activities yourself. There is a button that allows you to insert text boxes and in the same easy fashion pictures and films can be integrated.

Using IWB software for creating materials

Although for the simple material below no more than a chalk board or an overhead projector would really be necessary, creating it for the interactive whiteboard has the advantage that you are already prepared when you start the lesson and the activity is completely reusable as you just have to wipe away the added circles with the virtual sponge. On the right hand side one can see all the other pages of the file. By just tapping on them, one can flip from one page to the other.

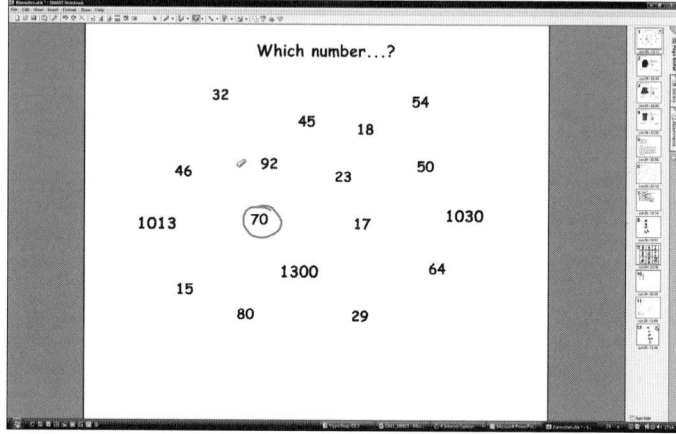

Screenshot 6.13: A simple text based activity created with the Notepad software of the Smartboard

A big gallery of pictures and backgrounds is included in the software and inserting pictures from the internet works through the normal cut and paste process. In most software packages you find a timer as well as virtual dice within the gallery. The timer counts down and indicates when the time is up which is a help for students as they can check their timing during an activity and a good device for keeping the pace of the lesson at the right level. The dice are ideal for games that are played within the whole class.

The screen shade and spotlight functions

Another function is the screen shade that, once activated, hides the whole screen. This serves the same purpose as the old-fashioned pieces of paper that are used on overhead projectors in order to hide parts of a transparency. In screenshot 6.14 it is used in order to simply display parts of a picture, e.g. for a simple

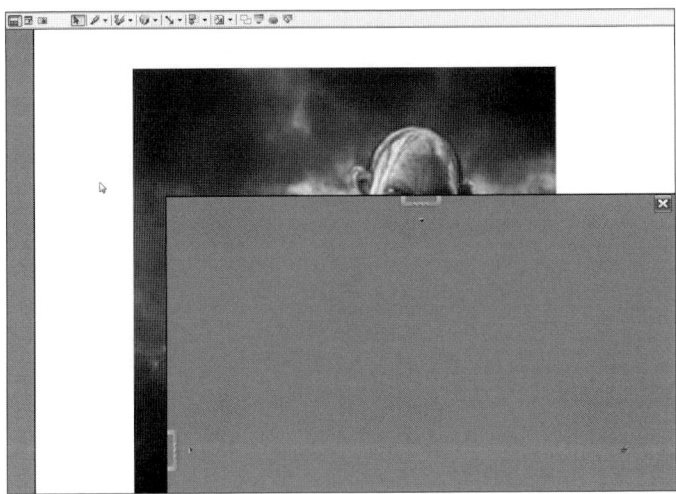

Screenshot 6.14: The curtain function of the Smartboard software

guessing game. For this purpose one could alternatively use the spotlight function which keeps the whole screen in black and only shows the part that one chooses to highlight by moving the curser across the screen. Also, the whole picture could be covered by different shapes that one creates with the programme and places on top of the picture – in a guessing game these shapes can be removed one after the other.

There are many more options for designing pages within the software. With a bit of preparation beforehand this means that you might not have to write and create as much within the lesson. This is obviously only true for contents that can be prepared beforehand and will not need to be created within the lesson. While a lot of these teacher led activities certainly motivate the students if used sporadically, one has to take care not to overuse the interactive whiteboard in this teacher centred way.

For a more student-centred approach one can buy additional applications, such as interactive slates that students can write on and that communicate with the interactive whiteboard. Several people or groups can work on their slates at the same time and can send their results to the board for a presentation. Also, there are interactive response gadgets for interactive whiteboards that look a bit like mobile phones and that allow the people equipped

Student centred usage of the IWB

with them to take part in quizzes and polls in the classroom just by pressing buttons. The teacher can carry out surveys or play quizzes, within groups or with each student voting or playing by him- or herself. Those tools are ideal for authentic discussions on important issues, for evaluations of classroom work and also for an overview of how much the class knows on a given topic. While the response tool will mostly be of importance at the beginning or at the end of a project or unit, the interactive slates will be used in more productive and creative phases.

6.6 Focus on Research

What kind of attitudes towards IWB technology would you expect learners of English to have?

Despite lots of promising and advanced tools there is not much genuine research in the area of using authoring tools or electronic whiteboards. One notable exception is a study on the use of authoring tools by advanced language learners who created interactive activities based on the Authoring Suite (see 6.2). The study indicates that students are capable of using such tools if the authoring process is guided by the teacher. Peer-generated materials (which need to be checked by the teacher) can be highly stimulating and efficient for the learning process (Ritter 1994: 351 ff.).

Using the voting system of the IWB

There is also a recent extensive study on the potential of electronic whiteboards for language teaching (Cutrim Schmid 2009). Cutrim Schmid did not only look at different possibilities for using electronic whiteboards in lessons, she also examined the type of interactions the different uses triggered and surveyed the students' attitudes towards using the device. So while the voting device, for example, was generally seen as enriching for the classroom, students also saw the limitations and downsides of using such a device. Table 6.4 summarizes the educational benefits of using the voting system in connection with the electronic whiteboard and also the challenges and problems that were found.

Pros of using the voting system	Challenges in connection with using the voting system
– increased level of student participation – instant feedback for the teacher – possibility for students to check their progress and standing within the group – increase of student's thinking time – assessing students' initial understanding before discussing a topic – raising students' curiosity before introducing a topic in detail – stimulating debates on subjective issues – element of fun through the design of competition games	– constant guessing as a negative factor (student criticism), sometimes in connection with lack of subsequent clarification – Learner anxiety when anonymity is not granted (e.g. if students know each others' panel numbers) – Limitation of student participation, e.g. through the format of multiple choice questions, large amount of teacher talk prior to voting, teacher centeredness through mostly teacher initiated questions – Peer influence during the voting system

Table 6.4: Pros and cons of the voting system of interactive White-boards (summarized from Cutrim Schmid 2009: 157-208)

It is interesting to see that although students perceived the voting system to be stimulating and enriching in general, they also found that the way the system was used was actually narrowing down their options for participation as the lessons were very reliant on the prepared materials and the teacher's input. So there was a wish, for example, to integrate more free discussions in order to be able to develop ideas within a conversation (2009:198ff.). The researcher also observes that, although the use of the voting system seemed more interactive at first sight, the interaction pattern was very repetitive, with a recurring cycle of teacher initiated questions, students' responses and teacher initiated analysis of results (2009: 200). Cutrim Schmid suggests that by exploiting the results more, e.g. by using them as a lead in for an extensive class-based discussion or by using the voting system after a longer discussion in class, this pattern could be broken up (2009: 201f.).

Cutrim Schmid's research results are very much in line with the impression we got from using electronic whiteboards in the classroom ourselves. It is very tempting to use electronic whiteboards in a teacher centred way, also because the materials one can find or create are very attractive as first sight but have to be managed by the one who chose them. Apart from the challenge of mastering the technology, the main challenge for teachers and practitioner researchers certainly lies in developing methods and tasks that ensure a maximum of involvement on the learners' side.

6.7 Classroom Ideas

Reflecting on what you have read in this chapter so far, how can you make use of the tools described to create games for your classes?

Just like in previous chapters there have been classroom ideas within this chapter already, so that we have decided to focus on some *how-to* information in this part rather than on presenting an elaborated lesson idea.

Creating interactive games with PowerPoint

We would like to share with you how you can produce an interactive and personalized PowerPoint quiz for your students. Although this is a teacher led activity, those kinds of quizzes can be personalized to a great extent in order to meet the students' interests and could also refer, for example, to joint prior experiences, such as a class trip.

Screenshot 6.15: An interactive game created with PowerPoint for the use on interactive whiteboards

Screenshot 6.15 shows what the first page of such a game could look like. Your students will have the impression that this is the only page they see while really you are clicking through a straightforward PowerPoint presentation as screenshot 6.16 shows.

Screenshot 6.16: The succession of slides as a basis for the interactive whiteboard game

Screenshot 6.17: Colour codes of the interactive whiteboard game

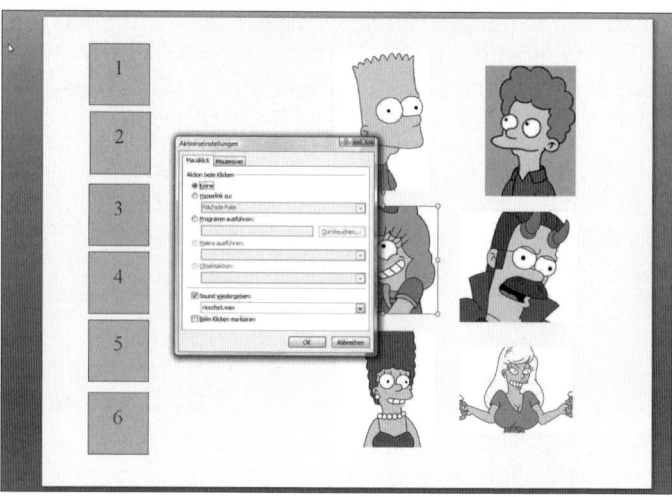

Screenshot 6.18: Customizing the interactive whiteboard game

Screenshot 6.19: Customizing the interactive whiteboard game – sound effects

Screenshot 6.20: A PowerPoint based Jeopardy game about Australia created by Sascha Gruenewald, a (former) student at the University of Duisburg-Essen

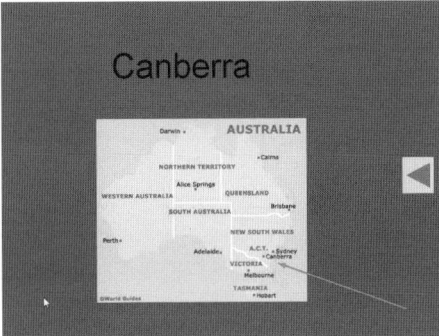

Screenshots 6.21 and 6.22: Sample task and answer of the Jeopardy game

The game displayed here is a simple matching activity. Oral descriptions of characters, in this case the Simpsons, which have been hyperlinked with the numbered squares, have to be matched with the pictures on the right. In this case the presentation that has been created for the game is linear, which means that the numbers have to be clicked on one after the other. In order to show students which number to click on next, one can highlight the current number with a different colour (see screenshot 6.17).

The files that one might want to hyperlink with the square, could, in this case either be an authentic sound file taken from a film clip or a self-recorded one that has been saved into the same folder as the presentation.

In order to hyperlink the sound file (or any other file or PowerPoint slide) with the squares, one has to right click and can then choose from different options.

During the presentation clicking on the square will then activate the hyperlink and the sound file is played, more than once if needed. In the game which is displayed here, we will now only need a feedback that shows students whether they have chosen the right option. This can be done by hyperlinking the pictures on the right with a sound. There are many different sounds to choose from, e.g. applause for a right answer and a beeping sound for a wrong answer. In this slide only one picture will obviously be hyperlinked with applause and the rest with a beeping sound. By clicking on any space on the screen that is not hyperlinked with a sound, you get to the next step of the quiz.

Tasks

1. Choose one of the authoring tools described in chapter 6.2 or a different authoring tool that you know and create a sample activity with it (for Puzzlemaker you do not need to download a programme). Be prepared to talk about the process of creating the activity and about your teaching idea.

2. Follow any of the links provided in chapter 6.3 in order to inform yourself about the different types of diagnosis and assessment. Then talk to a partner about your ideas of what diagnosis and assessment in English lessons should be like. Discuss ideal solutions as well as the constraints you see.

3. Follow the links on e-portfolios to get general information.
   a) Together with a partner create a structure of an e-portfolio that would be able to cater for all types of work and assessment that is done in English lessons.
   b) What kind(s) of programme(s) would you use for the e-portfolio?

4. How could a learning management system, such as Moodle, help you with diagnosis and assessment? Where do you see potentials and limitations?

5. Visit the website of any provider of electronic whiteboards and see what new developments there are in addition to the ones described in this chapter. What potentials for language teaching do you see in those features?

6. Drawing on your knowledge of what one can use electronic whiteboards for, come up with a classroom idea that is student centred and leaves room for students' ideas. Be prepared to present it in class.

7. Create a quiz using presentation software, following the steps described in chapter 6.7. For an additional idea for a format see screenshots 6.19, 6.20 and 6.21 of a jeopardy quiz about Australia, created by Sascha Grunewald, a student at the University of Duisburg-Essen.

TUTORIAL COURSEWARE | 7

7.1 Overview

To what extent can computers take over teaching functions, i.e. become tutors in the learning process?

Tool vs. tutor In this chapter we are going to explore the tutorial role of the computer. As we briefly indicated in the history of CALL (see ch. 1.2) it has repeatedly been suggested that a rough distinction between the computer as a tutor should be made vs. the computer as a tool. While the tool metaphor refers to all 'open' functions that digital media can be used for in the learning process (e.g. writing texts, looking up words, listening to audio files), the function as a tutor is more narrowly defined: Here the computer acts as a learning and teaching 'partner', provides explicit teaching materials, analyses learner input and offers feedback, or makes suggestions as to what the user should do next.

The computer as a digital teacher Clearly, the tool function is, on the whole, the more important one, simply because it reflects what computers are there for anyway – as tools that enable us to do things which would be impossible or more difficult to do without them. In that respect, all chapters in this book so far mainly emphasize this tool perspective (e.g. search engines, chat programs, blogs etc. are all tools which are 'open' with regard to content, and do not have an explicit tutorial function). On the other hand, should the potential of the computer as a teaching and learning device be dismissed altogether? In the history of CALL, many efforts were made to establish the computer as a 'digital teacher', and enthusiasts believed that computers would soon take over the job of teaching. A lot of research was dedicated to making such tutorial software more flexible and more adaptive to the individual learner's needs. There are various reasons why this euphoria has somewhat worn off in recent years: First, the Internet and its various tools have proven to be so powerful and promising for the language classroom that much of the research and development has gone into this field, and second, the quality of the tutorial software was often less than perfect and progress with regard to 'software intelligence' a lot slower than expected. Furthermore, tutorial software had (and still has) an unfavourable image among some researchers and teachers, who associate such software with monotonous drill and practice patterns or outdated memorization of grammar rules. Hubbard has investigated this negative image in more detail in his article "Another look at tutorial CALL" (2004), and unmasked many of these reservations as unjustified myths. They argue that there has been considerable progress in the development of such software, and that tutorial and tool uses of the computer can often complement each other in innovative ways.

We also believe that a book on teaching English with computers would be incomplete without a chapter on tutorial software. Having said this, it is quite a challenge to classify this heterogeneous field into manageable units. Traditional categories are becoming increasingly blurred – e.g. tutorial software being delivered offline on CD-Rom or DVD's versus tool software which is largely online. Another plausible categorization of tutorial software is to draw a line between self-access software for individual use and classroom software which can be dealt with in larger groups (i.e. in the classroom). This is the classification we are following here. First, we are investigating self-access software which has been developed by textbook-publishers and is linked to the course books that are in use in German schools (7.2). In a second step we are going to look at software which offers digital language learning environments for adults primarily and which is often more innovative than current school solutions (7.3). Finally, we are looking at emerging software trends of integrating tutorial software into the language classroom (7.5).

Classification of software products

7.2 Textbook-related courseware

How 'digital' will course materials be in ten years' time, and how will that affect classroom procedures?

Since the widespread availability of personal computers in the Nineties, all textbook publishers have started offering accompanying software products for their major course books. Typically, these programs offer separate vocabulary and grammar learning activities (*Vokabel- und Grammatiktrainer*), plus possibly reading and listening comprehension exercises. Such materials have been (and still are) advertised for more private use outside the language classroom, and many parents will have purchased such software in an attempt to improve their children's grades or to replace more expensive private tuition by software.

One such example is the English Coach series which accompanies the various English course books by Cornelsen. The screenshot below offers an idea of the learning areas that are typically integrated in such software.

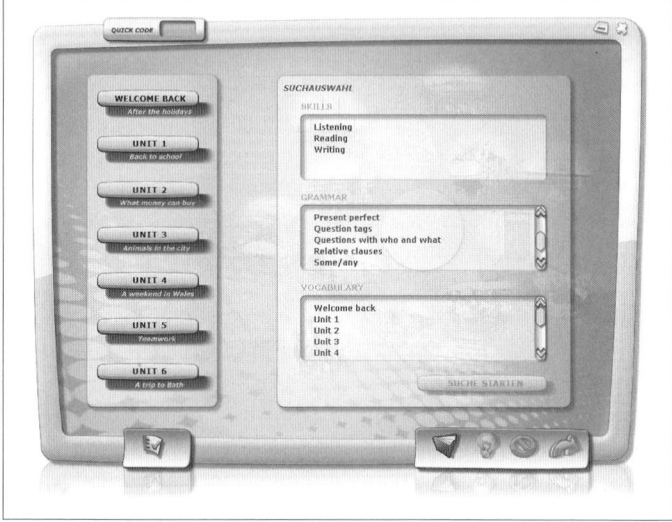

Screenshot 7.1: English Coach, overview of learning areas

As indicated above, a decisive question with regard to such software is its tutorial nature, i.e. its ability to "interact" with the learner.

Only a handful of teachers have integrated such programs into their lessons, for example by devoting some lesson time to individual work in the school's computer lab.

What is evident is that methods and materials must meet highest standards if teachers, learners, parents and politicians are to be convinced about a move in such a direction. Various instruments are available to explore the quality of existing software packages, e.g. the renowned German prize 'digita' which is awarded annually to honour the most innovative and promising developments. A look into the criteria that the digita jury has set up reveals the following three points of reference:

<Adaptivität, Interaktivität, Medialität > (see www.digita.de, Kriterien)

Criteria for evaluating software products

Looking at courseware from these three perspectives, the following questions could be asked:

- How 'adaptive' is the software to the learners' needs? Is the content in line with what the learner requires to move on in his/her learning? Is the target group of the software explicitly identified? Can learners make selections from different profiles or opt for different learning paths? Does the software compile and store results of the learner's progress and make suggestions for further learning?
- How 'interactive' is the software? What kind of feedback is provided? Does it go beyond 'wrong – try again' in case of errors, e.g. differentiate between typing errors and 'real' errors? Can learners choose between different levels of difficulty? Does the software make suggestions about what to do next?
- Does the software use its media-related possibilities to the fullest potential? How are text, sound, images or videos integrated? Are the design and ergonomics (the human-computer interface) user-friendly? What is the range of activities – how creative are tasks with regard to user input (i.e. more than gap-filling and multiple choice)?

Various evaluation forms have been developed to help users assess the worth of a particular piece of software. Below is such an evaluation form from the website ict4lt.org which also covers some of the questions asked above:

Title of software package / program:	
Criterion	
Is the level of language that the program offers clearly indicated?	Yes/No
Is it easy to start the program?	Yes/No
Is the user interface easy to understand? (For example, is the screen layout clear and easy to interpret?)	Yes/No
Is it easy to navigate through the program?	Yes/No
Are icons that are used to assist navigation (e.g. back to the homepage, exit) clear and intelligible?	Yes/No

Is it always clear to the learner which point s/he has reached in the program?	Yes/No
Does the program include scoring?	Yes/No
If a scoring system is used, does it make sense?	Yes/No
If a scoring system is used, does it encourage the learner?	Yes/No
Is the learner offered useful feedback if s/he gets something wrong?	Yes/No
If the learner gets something right purely by chance, can s/he seek an explanation in order to find out why the answer is right?	Yes/No
Can the learner seek help, e.g. on grammar, vocabulary, pronunciation, cultural content?	Yes/No
Does the program branch to remedial routines?	Yes/No
Can the learner easily quit something that is beyond his/her ability?	Yes/No
Are the grammar and vocab used in the program accurate?	Yes/No
Does the program offer cultural insights?	Yes/No
If the program includes pictures, are they (a) relevant, (b) an aid to understanding?	Yes/No
If the program includes sound recordings, are they of an adequate quality?	Yes/No
If the program includes sound recordings, are they (a) relevant, (b) an aid to understanding?	Yes/No
If the program includes sound recordings, is there a good mix of male and female voices and regional variations?	Yes/No
Can the learner record his/her own voice and play it back?	Yes/No
Does the program make use of Automatic Speech Recognition (ASR)?	Yes/No
If the program makes use of ASR, is it effective?	Yes/No
If the program includes video sequences, are they of an adequate quality?	Yes/No
If the program includes video sequences, are they (a) relevant, (b) an aid to understanding?	Yes/No
Is the program relevant to your national / regional / departmental programme of study?	Yes/No

Table 7.1: A Software Evaluation Form (taken from www.ict4lt.org, module 1.4)

The focus of this sub-chapter has been on textbook-related courseware. Naturally, such criteria can also be applied to text-book-independent courseware which we will look at next.

7.3 Textbook-independent courseware

How will human-computer interaction develop in the future?

Tutorial courseware which does not come with a particular coursebook is often aimed at adults who want to or need to brush up their language skills. Probably, most adults still tend to resort to language schools, private coaching, audio materials and books to improve their language competence, but the digital market is continually expanding, and existing materials have made remarkable progress in the last ten or 15 years. One such program is the 'Tell Me More' series (TMM) which we would like to take as an example of this type of software to demonstrate some its most notable features (see task at the end of this chapter for a further example).

Since adult learners often have difficulties assessing their current level of language competence, such software offers a diagnostic or assessment test at the outset. Most programs follow the levels suggested by the 'Common European Framework of Reference for Languages' (CEFR), which identifies six different stages, from A1 to C2. TMM translates the CEFR stages into ten levels (see screenshot 7.2).

In the following, TMM lets learners choose between a guided mode based on a pre-defined path through lessons and units, or a 'free-to-roam' mode which leaves it to the user to choose activities. Besides more traditional tasks like gap-filling or multiple choice exercises on vocabulary and grammar, learners can also take over a role in a 'virtual dialogue' and 'interact' with virtual characters in a given situation.

Here, the technology of 'speech recognition' comes into play when the software tries to recognize spoken words that the user produces through a microphone. Obviously, this is a non-trivial task since the user's sound waves have to be analysed and matched with sound patterns stored in a database.

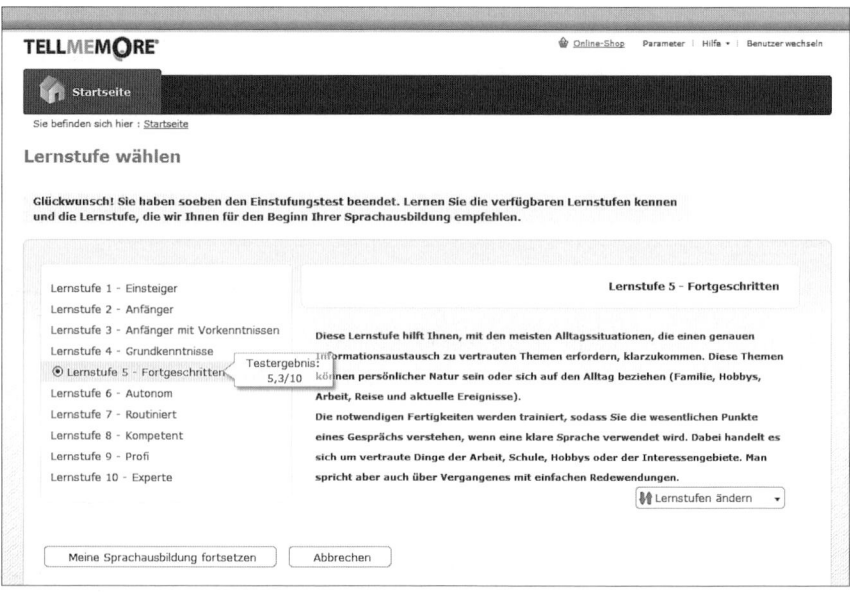

Screenshot 7.2: Online diagnostic test in TMM – here: result page

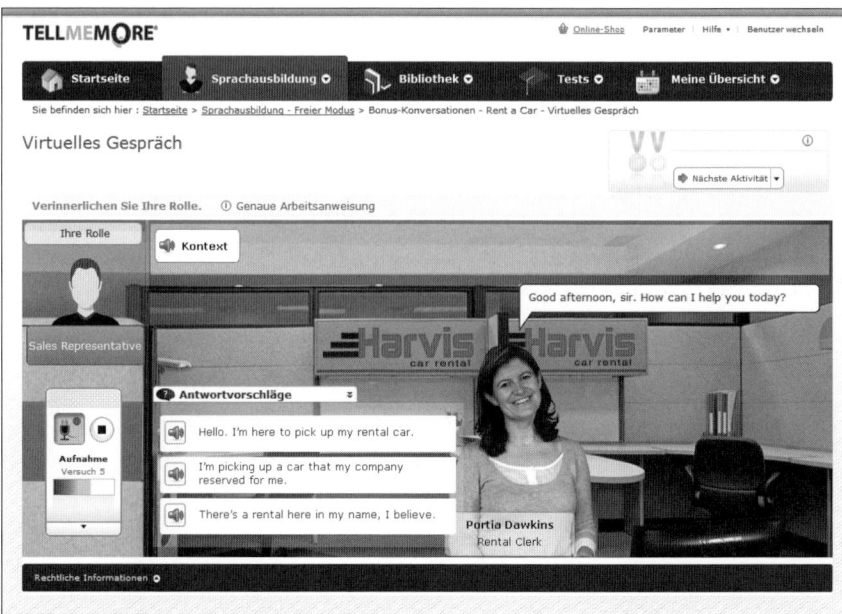

Screenshot 7.3: Virtual dialogue in TMM based on speech recognition

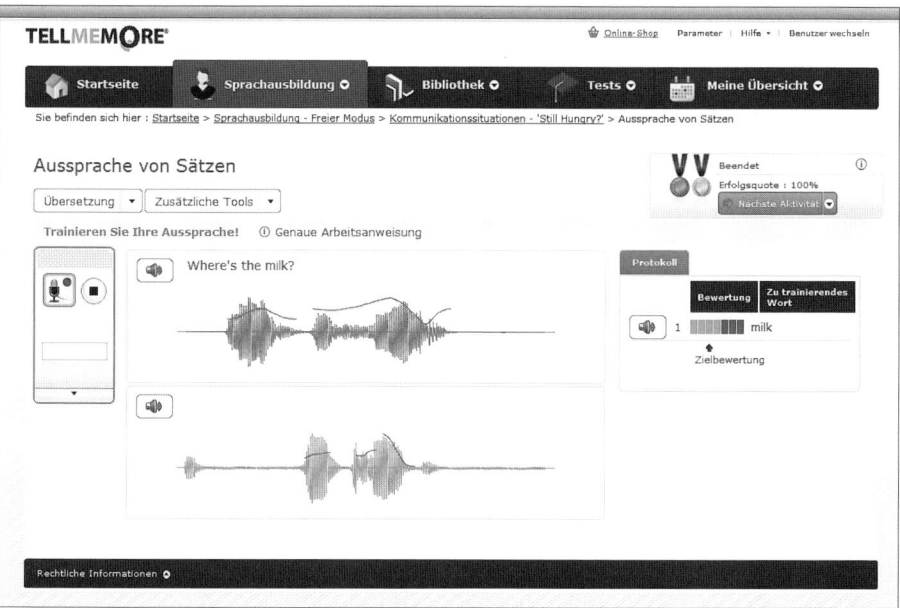

Screenshot 7.4: Pronunciation activity in TMM based on speech analysis

The same technology is used in another area of TMM to practise the articulation of words or sentences.

The learning benefit of such tasks is debatable, and some learners will undoubtedly profit more from such a 'technical' approach to phonology than others. However, the range of activities and approaches that software like TMM offers is remarkable and becoming more and more diversified, catering for the individual needs of different learners. At the same time, a real teacher or tutor will always remain more 'adaptive' and 'interactive', and tutorial software cannot fully replace human empathy. It is therefore not a matter of replacing human tutoring and instruction, but rather assisting and supporting it through digital media.

7.4 Focus on Research

How do learners perceive the use of computers in the language class-room – are digital media really more motivating in the long run?

Surprisingly little research has been done in the field of tutorial courseware over the years. While commercial developing companies and publishing houses have been busy developing more sophisticated courseware, these products have not received much empirical or theoretical attention. This might also have to do with the unfavourable image of tutorial software that we briefly outlined above (see 7.1).

A look into the archive of the online journal 'Language Learning & Technology' reveals a few studies that investigate the learning potential of multimedia courseware. For instance, Al-Seghayer (2001) investigates the effects that different multimedia modalities (text only, still image, video) have on the learning of new words, Grgurovic & Hegelheimer (2007) analyse in a similar study the impact of subtitles and transcripts on listening comprehension, or Murphy (2007) looks into online reading comprehension tasks and the effects of pair work vs. individual work.

One of the few more comprehensive studies on the use of tutorial software tasks was conducted by Schmidt (2007). In his longitudinal study Schmidt integrated the software English Coach 2000 (a predecessor of English Coach 21, see 7.2) into an intermediate English language classroom. While the software is primarily designed for individual work, it was largely used in pair work for the purposes of this study. Based on video recordings, learner diaries, questionnaires and interviews, here are some of Schmidt's central conclusions: tutorial courseware can lead to significant negotiation of meaning in front of the screen (when done in pair work); the software in question can be improved with regard to its interface design and ergonomics; corrective feedback is highly valuable for the learning process if it is differentiated enough; tutorial courseware can be the springboard for more complex classroom activities; teachers need special training to develop expertise in integrating CALL-related activities.

With regard to textbook-independent courseware, Nandorf (2004) analysed how adult learners use such programs individually. Among other courseware titles, she also integrated an earlier version of 'Tell Me More' (see 7.3) in her study. Her many findings cannot be summarized adequately here, but some of her conclusions seem to confirm what we stated above: tutorial courseware can be a powerful tool for individual learning, and learners often have high expectations and a high degree of motivation when using such tools. However, this motivation can wear off quickly if the software isn't adaptive and interactive enough to adjust to the learners' needs, or if learners feel overwhelmed with the many options that the software offers. In the end, Nandorf concludes, tutorial courseware is no complete substitute for the social dimension of language learning in a group of learners, guided by a tutor.

Future research in this field could follow up on studies like the ones by Schmidt or Nandorf: which types of tasks lend themselves to successful 'interaction' between the software and the user (see 'task design' in 3.4)? Why do some learners make more use of the complex options that modern tutorial courseware offers than others (i.e. individual differences and learning styles)? How can tutorial software become more 'intelligent' to adapt to individual learners and their preferences?

Research questions like these can shed more light on the efficiency of tutorial courseware and eventually lead to learning environments with digital components which facilitate the language learning process.

7.5 Classroom Ideas

How well-equipped with digital media are schools in Germany today? What is the situation like in schools that you know?

Digital courseware can be implemented in the classroom in various scenarios. Teachers can display the screen of a tutorial program via a data projector or an interactive whiteboard ('interaktives Tafelbild', see 6.5), and work through a particular activity together with their students. A more ambitious and more student-centred scenario is situated in a computer lab where students work individually or share a computer. The 'Unterrichtssoftware' based on the coursebook English G 21 (see 7.2) offers a pathway for both scenarios and is taken here as an example of coursebook-related work with tutorial software. While the 'lead-ins' of each unit lend themselves to the more teacher-controlled scenario (projector, whiteboard), there are a number of so-called 'mini projects' which take up the major themes of each coursebook unit. As way of example, unit 4 in English G 21 A2 (grade 6) focuses on students' descriptions of recent activities ('sagen, was man gerade/schon/noch nicht gemacht hat'), and thereby introduces the present perfect tense. Accordingly, the mini project of the accompanying software consists of an interactive quiz called '10 things you've always wanted to know'. With the help of a 'Story Machine' students answer questions about themselves.

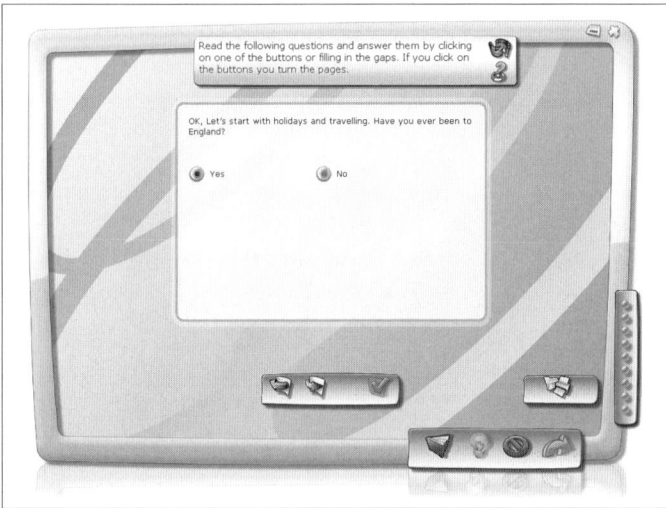

Screenshot 7.5: Question from mini project, in 'Unterrichtssoftware English G 21 A2, Unit 4'

After answering a number of such questions, the Story Machine generates a short text about each student which can be printed and used for various forms of classroom activities (e.g. 'Find somebody who ...').

The major grammar aspect of this unit, the present perfect, can be practised in a more form-focused activity before or after the quiz, depending on the students' needs and previous knowledge.

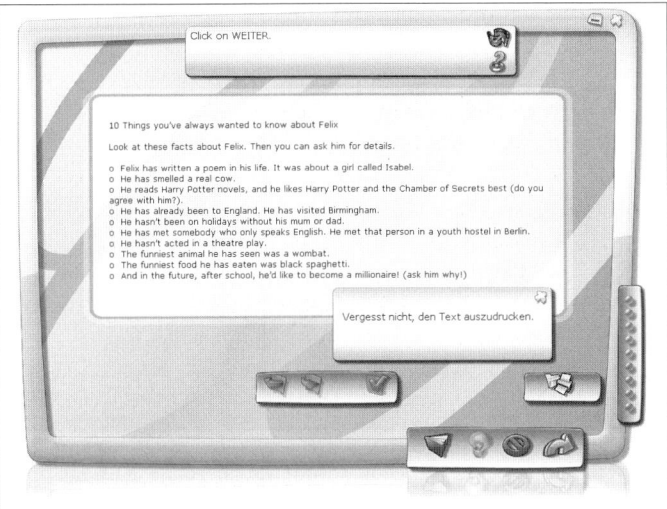

Screenshot 7.6: Sample text result of the mini project

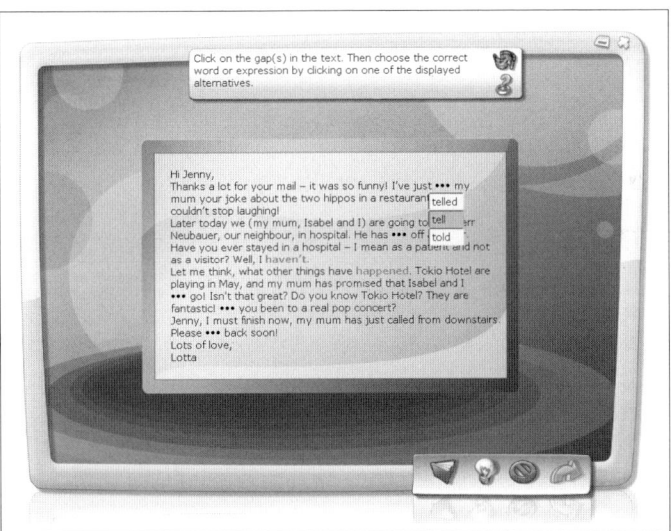

Screenshot 7.7: Text-based multiple choice exercise, as part of the mini project

As with any lesson planning, it is up to the teacher how to combine meaning- and form-focused sequences. Digital courseware significantly adds to the options that teachers have to turn the language classroom into a rich learning environment.

Tasks

1. Have a look at one of the available textbook-related courseware titles (demo versions are usually available for free). Against the background of this chapter, how do you judge them? Would you like to work with them as a learner?
2. Go to www.digita.de and look at the award-winning software programs of the last years.
3. Go to www.digitalpublishing.de, one of the leading German publishers of tutorial courseware for language learning, and get an overview of the existing software series (various demos and video trailers are available).
4. Go to the portal 'Information and Communications Technology for Language Teachers' (www.ict4lt.org), and familiarize yourself with module 2.2, 'Introduction to multimedia CALL' (left frame: Contents).
5. Familiarize yourself with the 'Common European Framework of Reference for Languages' (CEFR). What are the six levels of competence specified there?

SOCIAL SOFTWARE | 8

8.1 Overview

How has the web changed since the first time you used it?

The World Wide Web and the way it is used have changed a lot since Tim Berners-Lee, the founder of the web as we know it today, published the first site in 1992. The great new idea back then was that documents from all over the world should be linkable through the use of the same code, i.e. http, which means hypertext transfer protocol, and all users of the internet should be able to view them with the help of a specific kind of software, so-called explorers. In this way a world wide web of hyperlinked documents developed. As we all know, the impact of this work has been immense and has resulted in a whole new era that has often been called information age because of the vast amount of information that is available to everyone online.

Developments of the www

The web has developed much further since then. More storage space on- and offline, faster internet connections, additional kinds of codes and user-friendly software make it easy for everyone not only to find information online but also to produce and publish materials themselves, i.e. the web nowadays is not a read-only web for the common user as it was in the early days but a read-and-write web. One of the biggest positive effects of this development is a democratization of the contents of the www, i.e. everyone can be an author now and can have his or her voice heard. When we look at picture 8.1 below, we will see that this positive effect is always balanced by other forces, such as manipulation through commercial control, the social pressure of peer groups to use certain apps if one wants to be part of the in-group and, in some contexts, also control through censorship. Without neglecting these negative forces, we will primarily focus on the potential that some of the social software tools have for teaching and learning English in this publication.

There are a lot of applications for creating and publishing materials, such as wikis, blogs or podcasts that can be utilized for language teaching and learning. The great potential of these applications is that they are social in nature, i.e. the materials produced are published in order to be viewed and commented on by an audience or, as it is the case with wikis, even to be co-

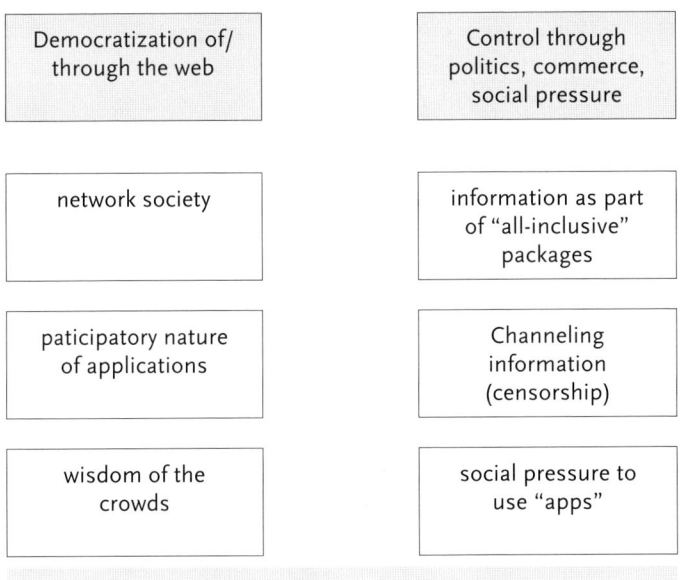

Democratization of/ through the web	Control through politics, commerce, social pressure
network society	information as part of "all-inclusive" packages
paticipatory nature of applications	Channeling information (censorship)
wisdom of the crowds	social pressure to use "apps"

Picture 8.1: Concurring trends connected with technological developments

constructed by either the general public or a pre-defined group of people. These applications, which invite people to share materials and exchange views, are called social software, the web of people and documents that is created through the use of these applications is referred to as social web (see Richardson 2009). In this chapter we are going to highlight how some of these applications can be made use of but, as already indicated above, will also focus on critical issues which are relevant for the safety and general sanity of your future students.

8.2 Talking Terms: Social Software vs. Web 2.0

How do you think the terms Social Software and Web 2.0 are related?

Collective intelligence

As already outlined at the beginning of this chapter, applications, such as wikis, blogs or social networks, can be subsumed under the term social software. Social software enables users of the web to interact with each other, to co-construct meaning and to produce as well as view materials online. This read and write state of the web is also often referred to as web 2.0, however, expressing the idea that the whole nature of the web and the way it is used has changed since the day it came into being. The term has become a bit of a buzz word but its meaning is still quite fuzzy. With ongoing developments people are starting to discuss whether the changes at the time of writing can still all be summarized under the term web 2.0 or whether we are already entering the stage of web 2.5 or can even see the stage of web 3.0 emerging already. As those labels that refer to the alleged stages of the web are likely to change and do not say anything about the nature of the changes that are taking place, we prefer to use the more descriptive terms social software and social web in this publication.

8.3 Wikis

If the most well-known set of wikis is Wikipedia – how would you then describe what a wiki is?

Wikis are online documents which can be co-created by a group of people, often by the general public. The term wiki comes from the Hawaiian term *wiki-wiki* and means quick which refers to the fact that wikis can be created and adapted quickly. The most well-known wiki, Wikipedia (see chapter 4.4), is still a wiki that invites everyone to participate but it is now watched by appointed editors who delete articles that do not meet the standards. Wikis in general rely on the power of co-creation and –construction. Everyone is a potential author or editor. The vision behind this is a very

democratic and empowering one: We are not reliant on the information the press and others provide us with – we share the
power of what is published and how it is published with everyone
else who has got internet access. Every statement that seems too
radical or just untrue can be deleted or edited and if we think a
topic or event deserves a new entry, we can start creating it and
see how others join in. The aim is to produce an entry that gets
the widest possible acceptance.

There are many wiki tools available, a lot of them for free.
Some well-known software products are *Wikispaces*, *PBWiki* and
MediaWiki. Also, wikis are often integrated into other services.
Content management systems, for example, such as *Moodle* or
Ilias (see chapter 6.4), all offer the option of incorporating wikis
into the online modules. Within these systems the wikis will
normally only be used by a pre-defined group. This detracts from
the general idea and limits the power of public discourse but can
make sense in institutionalized contexts.

Wiki tools

The tools do differ in their functionality and the way they are
programmed. For example, some wikis require us to enter codes
in order to do the formatting, i.e. if we want to insert headlines
or want to italicise something, but some wikis are created in a
WYSIWYG (What you see is what you get) way, i.e. we mark a
headline, click on a button for turning it into bold type and see
the bold type of the headline on the screen. WYSIWYG programmes can be used intuitively as you can instantly see how the
changes will appear in the published version. The formatting
codes for other wikis are very simple to learn as well, however,
and give authors a little glimpse "behind the scenes" of how
software programmes normally function, i.e. through listing
codes. The extract from a tutorial shown in screenshot 8.1 shows
how the formatting of entries in wikis powered by MediaWiki, the
tool that is used by the Wikipedia Project, works.

Functionalities
of Wiki tools

There are different functions in the various wiki products but
some functions are shared by all of them. Everyone who has access
to the wiki – which depends on whether it is password secured or
not – can read the current state of the entries, so there is a fully
formatted version that doesn't differ much from other websites as
the wiki products allow for the integration of links, photos, films
and other files. Whether you need to register as a user in order to
be able to edit the sites can be defined under settings, i.e. the

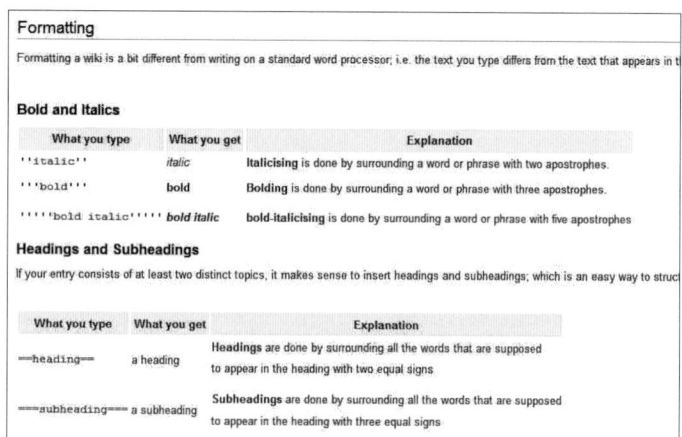

Screenshot 8.1: A tutorial for creating pages within a wiki (taken from: http://wiki.uni-due.de/ang)

administrators of the wiki can decide how open the wiki should be and can also define parts that cannot be changed by others. There is some fear among educators about opening up wikis to the public as the wiki is then also open to any kind of inappropriate use as well, such as deleting the entries of others or inserting inappropriate remarks or materials, that disturb the co-creation and that might cause parents to be against this public kind of work. One good thing is that all wikis do have a so-called history button (German: *Verlauf*) which allows us to see older versions, compare different versions and also to recover an older version if necessary. Thus, if the vandalism is not too extreme and persistent, the work that has been done by students will not be lost.

Also, if students are given responsibility for the maintenance of the wiki and develop a sense of ownership, they will often have an interest in dealing with any disturbing issues themselves. Still, opening up a wiki to the public might mean that parents are included in the decision making and that educational goals are made transparent.

Wikis can be used in many different ways in the classroom. A fairly simple use is illustrated in picture 8.2. University students reported on their research findings after having observed English lessons in different classes. As there were set parameters to look at, such as the number of display vs. real questions being used

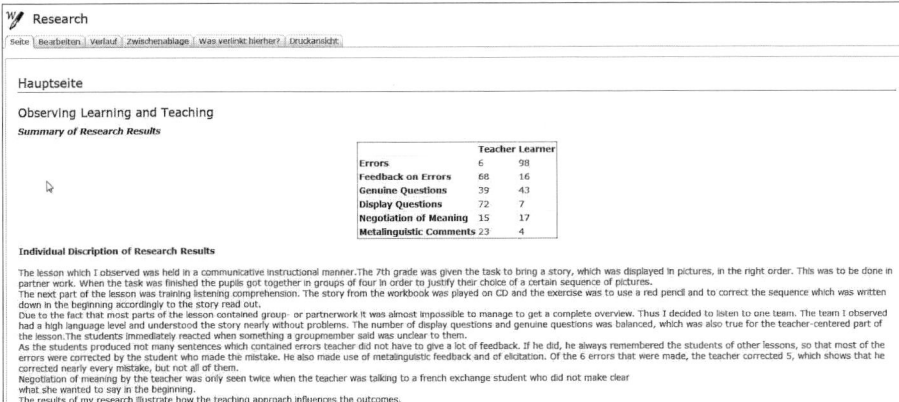

Screenshot 8.2: An extract from a wiki site created by students at the University of Marburg

in the lesson, each group could add numbers to a table that served as a basis for discussion in the next session. Below the list each group described their individual research results. Other uses of wikis at university level include the joint creation of a glossary with each student of a group defining a set number of terms, the joint task to suggest possible improvements or, for example, the task to evaluate different WebQuest in groups and publish the results in the same wiki.

There are wiki projects on all sorts of topics that students can contribute to. There is, for example, wikibooks that aims at creating free online resources for any kind of educational topic, there is a recipes wiki that everyone can add their own recipe box to and some cities have a wiki version of their website that everyone can add contents to.

8.4 Blogs and Microblogs

What do you use blogs for? And what reasons might people in general have for creating and keeping a blog?

The word blog is a contraction of the term weblog, which describes a log on the web. Blogging software enables people to create simple but visually appealing websites quickly enough in order to be able to keep others up to date through writing, sharing photos, web links, videos or any other kind of information. No knowledge of html or the use of specialist software is required for the creation of a weblog.

blogosphere The fact that blogs are easy to create has led to the production of large numbers of blogs on all spheres of life. Basically there is no topic that you will not find a blog on – there are more serious blogs with news and discussions on technical, medical, educational or political issues as well as sites on all sorts of hobbies or personal profiles of the people who created the blog. The whole entity of existing blogs that creates a big network of bloggers is called the blogosphere. The blogosphere is distinguished from the net of other websites in the following way:

characteristics of blogs But what really distinguishes a blog from your run-of-the-mill Website is much more than process; it's what you'll find there. Weblogs are not built on static chunks of content. Instead, they are comprised of reflections and conversations that in many cases are updated every day (if not three or four times a day). (Richardson 2009: 17f.)

There is no final product with blogging then as blogs, by nature, invite reflection and communication through the opportunity to post comments on the sites. Rather than just stating one's own view, finding a synthesis through dialogue could be seen as an ultimate aim of blogs (see Richardson 2009: 30). The really big potential of blogs then is that communities which share the same interest can communicate with each other in a meaningful way. The classroom can be seen as such a community and blogs can help this community to organise their work more efficiently, to discuss relevant topic related issues or to interact with other communities.

blogs as a class portal Work in a class can be organized through a blog, i.e. teachers can publish work to do, news and organizational aspects through a blog; students and parents then could subscribe to these news through RSS (see chapter 6.2) and could be invited to discuss certain aspects together with the teacher. For examples of blogs used by English teachers in order to publish plans, procedures and assignments, see Donath's site (schule.de/englisch/blogs. htm) which provides a good collection of different approaches on blogging in and for English lessons.

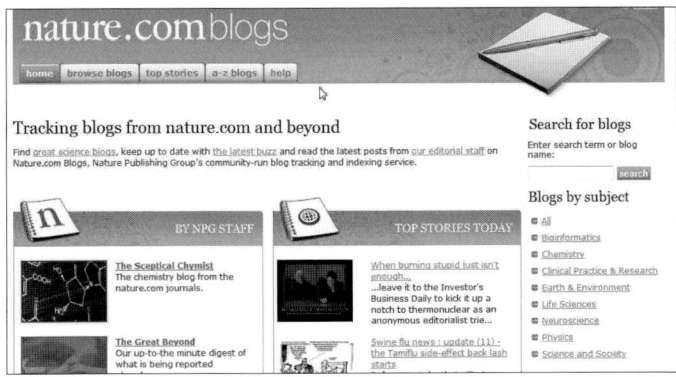

Screenshot 8.3: Screenshot from a blog with news and critical discussions on nature and natural sciences (taken from nature.com)

In languages lessons weblogs can, for example, accompany the work with a book or a film, e.g. through the presentation and discussion of the main characters, important background information, the discussion of critical issues and the presentation of creative work done. In this way all the work is published, can be used for further reference in class and can also be read by people who are interested in the book. Screenshot 8.4 shows a screenshot of a reading log created during a project of the University of Duisburg-Essen and class 9b at the Burggymnasium in Essen.

blogs for topic related issues

The kind of blog that we can see in picture 8.4 could be used for any kind of project or topic based work to show its results to the public. It can also be used for further work, e.g. for triggering a conversation on a particular topic. This particular case, shows the results of a project day at the University of Duisburg-Essen.

Students came up with new covers (see screenshot 8.6), worked on background information, created phone calls based on the book, and much more. For an overview of the categories that were worked on see screenshot 8.5.

In bilingual science lessons, for example, blogs on any of the topics that are discussed in the nature.com blog (see screenshot 8.3) can make classroom discourse authentic by inviting others to join in. Within this discussion the course can provide new or newly assembled information on the topic in question or can use

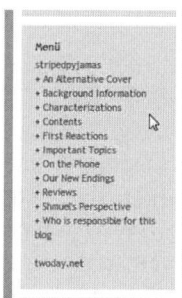

Screenshot 8.4: A snapshot from a reading log on John Boyne's The boy in the Striped Pyjamas (taken from: http://heimunidue.twoday.net/)

Screenshot 8.5: The contents of the blog on The boy in the striped pyjamas

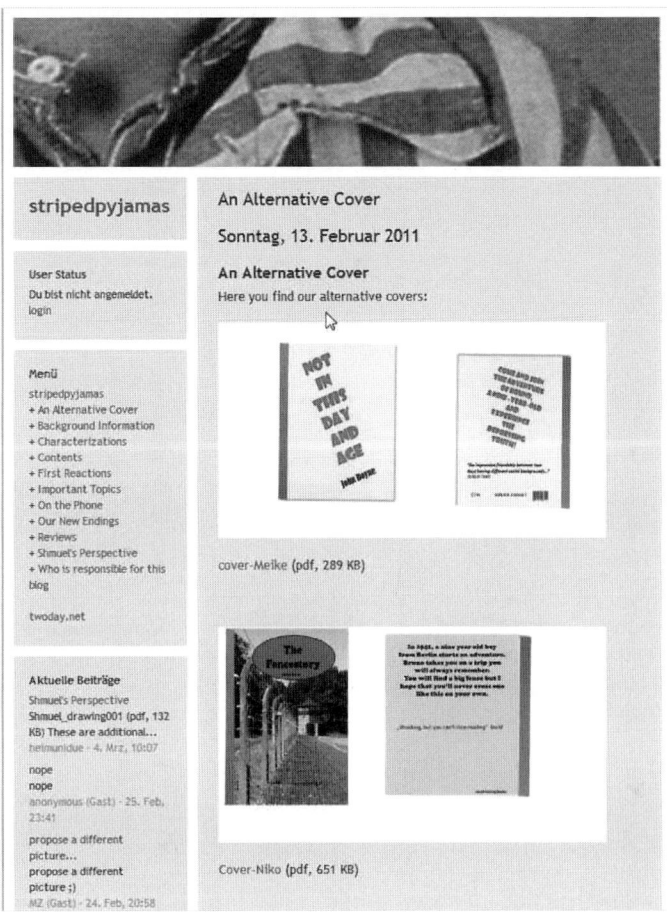

Screenshot 8.6: A display of the potential new covers that students created during the project day

the blog in order to interact with a partner class which is working on the same topic.

A great example of how to use weblogs for interaction with partner classes abroad is described by Ellermann (2009). In co-operation with a partner class in Australia she and her year six class sent a travel buddy, the German shepherd Horst, on his way to Brisbane where he was taken home by each member of the partner class. The culturally loaded experiences that the cuddly

blogs for encounter projects

toy made were always documented through photos and the students' task was also to come up with interesting questions that they could ask the students in their partner class about the pictures that were put online. In Germany the Australian koala Kate travelled around and also appeared online in many different situations. The students followed the entries with interest, and sent comments to the travel buddies, just like they would to a real person.

new writing genre   As you can see, work with blogs can take on about as many forms as working with other kinds of texts. It is a new writing genre, however, that does have its own rules and structures. Richardson (2009: 28) emphasises the open character as well as what is specific about blogging in the following way:

> Posting to a Weblog can take many forms. Students can write about personal reactions, to topics covered in class, post links, write reflectively, and summarise or annotate reading. They can use blogs as journals or as places to publish creative writing for larger audiences. The possibilities really are endless. But by their very structure, blogs facilitate what I think is a new form of genre and could be called "connective writing", a form that forces those who do it to read carefully and critically, that demands clarity and cogency in its construction that is done for a wide audience and that links to the sources of the ideas expressed.

new literacies   Blogs can and should also be used for gaining information in class, i.e. if students are to take their own work on blogs seriously, blogs should also be considered as a source to be taken seriously in general. As a blog is a new text type with a different culture than, for example, a printed newspaper article, students will have to develop additional literacy skills in order to be able to evaluate the materials they find. Rather than just evaluating an individual text, the whole network of information and views will have to be evaluated. The following steps might help to judge whether a source can safely be regarded as reliable or not:

1) Try to find out as much as you can about the authors (profession, title, authority on the topic,..).
2) Find out about the reputation the blogger has among his peers (e.g. by typing in the URL of the blog into the search function of the technorati.com site to see how many bloggers refer to the blog).

3) Look at the list of blogs that the blogger links to (reliability and views stated on those sites,..)
4) Reflect on the motivation of the blogger, apparent (political) views and level of reflection in order to judge how credible the source is.
(adapted from Richardson 2009: 37f.)

In this way, students will be encouraged to be critical and reflective and will develop a balanced view rather than, for example, just setting out to find blogs that might support their own view. Thus, working with blogs is a chance to develop a feeling for the importance of consulting different sources and using references for backing up one's own view. In this way students learn how to do research and how to judge research that is done by others. They learn that the credibility of blogs does not necessarily only rely on the authority of an individual author. The real quality of a blog can also be due to a collective intelligence that becomes apparent in the network of sources and in the way a synthesis is or is not found within a discussion.

Creating a blog for use in class is fairly straightforward. There is a lot of help online on how to set up a blog (see for example Donath's site) and the sites are mostly designed in a way that allows for intuitive use, so we will restrict ourselves to very basic information here. There are many sites where you can set up blogs for free. One of the most popular ones at the time of writing is wordpress.com, others are twoday or blogger.com. The first messages can be posted in the newly created blogs right after having received a welcome e-mail after registration. Basic forms of the blogs are usually for free. If you would like to have a advert free version or would like to upload larger amounts of data, you will have to pay a fee. If you would rather use a more institutionalized site you can try the blog function of the Lehrer-online platform *lo-net*. This is a platform that has especially been developed for use in schools and can thus be expected not to conflict with any educational goals.

Creating a blog

A trend with an unclear future at the time of writing is microblogging, i.e. the writing of short online memos, with one name being connected to this service: Twitter. The reason why this format was

Microblogs / Twitter

an instant success when it came into life is connected with the possibility of so-called followers being updated on any news that are posted by a particular author, in an interest group or on a specific topic, i.e. there is no need to search the web for news. Through smartphones which are connected to the internet people don't have to use their desktops or laptops in order to be able to get the messages. It's convenient for the author as he or she only has to worry about updating the blog in order to inform everyone who is interested. The messages are longer than short messages sent via mobile phone and can thus contain more substantial information; on the other hand they are concise enough to be readable more or less at a glance.

The site has been known to be used for business and journalistic purposes, i.e. for instantly informing a specific audience about new developments, but it has very quickly become popular for private use as well, with groups of people sharing information, photos and links. We generally do see a potential for using Twitter in order to keep oneself up to date regarding topics and areas of interest, e.g. if one follows what particular specialists in a field publish within Twitter and also for potentially connecting with those specialists. Actively encouraging advanced students to use Twitter might make sense for those purposes then, provided enough specialists make use of Twitter in order to connect with people in the future. For teachers, who are well connected internationally, using Twitter for receiving authentic comments on current affairs or on cultural aspects can be very useful. Even posting the question about what kinds of sports their followers like or what their favourite food is can be used in order to get authentic comments from native speakers or people who use the language as a lingua franca. These comments can then be used in class.

Educational responsibility

Asking students themselves to communicate via microblog, e.g. during project work, for example, can be very useful for developing their ability to write concise messages. If we encourage students to create and read blogs and microblogs, we also have the responsibility of discussing the netiquette, the dangers and pitfalls of using these tools. The power that the described tools can have in a positive way also leads to a big potential for misuse and for shedding a bad rather than a positive light on people. Services like Twitter or social networking sites make cyberbullying easier as messages about other people can be shared even more quickly than before. This is also shown by the suicides that are connected with cyberbulllying (see the extract from a Times-on-line report in screenshot 8.7). While bullying has always been there, the new technological developments make it easier for bullies to intrude into different spheres of life and to reach their potential victims wherever they are.

Screenshot 8.7: A Times-Online report on possible consequences of cyberbullying (21.09.09)

Another, also potentially hazardous tendency is for people to reveal a lot of personal information online. That this trend connected with the anonymity of the internet makes it easy for any kind of offender to get into contact with potential victims, is

Ideas for creating podcasts in English lessons

fortunately widely known already but might be dismissed with an "I am not that daft" if only uttered as a warning. There is very good material available for work on the topic at school though. The British government has produced a film, called *Jenny's Story*, based on the true story of a girl who revealed too much information while chatting to a stranger on msn and was almost killed as a consequence. While the message is very straight forward, it is the way in which Jenny tells her story that makes it effective and a good basis for classroom work.

People are now aware of the fact that companies often do gather more information about a potential employee than they could have gotten in the times before Facebook, StudiVZ and the like. Also, stories about people who are fired because of their overly revealing photos or comments in blogs or on social networking sites are appearing in the press. The private going public leads to more public control as well as to the great opportunity of linking with likeminded people from all over the world. While all this will hopefully be common knowledge for digital natives in the future, it might still be an interesting question to discuss "the modern complexities of social networking websites" (see the extract from Times-Online in screenshot 8.7) in class. There is already a distinct pressure to participate in business related networks as headlines like "Selbstmarketing: Mit Xing und Twitter Karriere machen" (Focus online: 4.8.09) show. Thus, provided things don't change dramatically, business as well as allegedly private social networks will have to be treated as a permanent portfolio of personal information.

8.5 Podcasting

What is the potential use of publishing students' video- and audio files on the web?

Podcasts have gained huge importance in language lessons over the last couple of years. They have already been mentioned as a great resource for language lessons in chapter 4 and as a great option for asynchronous online communication in chapter 3. In this context we are thus not going to focus on any detailed information regarding definitions and functionalities but will restrict ourselves to presenting additional uses for creating podcasts or videopodcasts in English lessons.

Creating a video or audio file in order to publish it on the internet afterwards, be it as part of a blog or on a site like YouTube, can be a great motivator for students as they know that they can potentially reach the broader public with their results.

A student group at the University of Duisburg-Essen once produced a video clip with a young adult group in which they copied the famous "Will it blend" ads. With the contents of the ads, in which a blender is filled with just about any kind of object that fits in, the question of health and safety as well as the ethical issue of willingly wasting valuable goods could be raised. With the particular student group in this project the amusing contents were as much of a motivator as the format of the production and the option of it possibly being published. Within the project the class was split up into the author group that came up with the texts, the technology group that dealt with any technical issues, such as filming and cutting the clip, the actors groups that acted within the clip and the "making-of" and reflection group that created a documentation of the whole project. In this way everyone was involved in some way and to some extent students' awareness of what it takes to produce a film was raised.

Other ideas for podcasts could, for example, be to create a film on a fictitious deleted scene from a drama in which the constellation of characters becomes clear or an interview with the characters including comments on a particular scene and characterizations of their character. This kind of work could also be a more holistic contribution to a blog on the drama or a piece of coursework that can be assessed.

Screenshot 8.8: A commercial site that was used as a basis for students' work (Taken from: http://www.blendtec.com/willitblend/)

Another option for a meaningful way of publishing students' work is the installation of a news podcast section on a school's homepage. This can take the format of the one- minute-news we often find on news portals or can be turned into a slightly longer news show. In order to be able to keep up this service regularly, forming an afternoon club is probably the best option. If you want to publish students' videos or audio files, parents' consent is always necessary if the students are under 18 years old. It might be wise to formulate and send out a consent form to parents at the beginning of the school year that covers all the work to be done with the group, so that parents are not flooded with consent forms throughout the year. Additionally, it would also be wise to address the issue at a parents' evening where parents have the chance to ask questions and where you might find it a lot easier to communicate your aims.

Some tools for creating podcasts have already been referred to in chapter 3.3. Another useful tool for creating and publishing podcasts (video- and audio) can be found on podomatic.com. This site can also help to find podcasts as a resource for lessons (see chapters 4 and 5).

8.6 Second Life

What is Second Life in your view?

Second life is a Multi User Virtual Environment (MUVE) which means that it can be used by a high number of people at the same time. In Second Life (SL) people act and interact within a three dimensional virtual world that is to a great extent created by the users themselves and which contains countries, cities, islands, casinos, shopping malls and all sorts of other amenities that we know from our real lives. Users move through this virtual world in the form of their chosen character or avatar, i.e. one could choose to be very much like one's real self or a completely new person, there can be references to characters one knows, one can be as young or old as one likes and one can aim to act out any kind of role within the virtual community – one can be the little daughter of an English speaking family, a member of a virtual sports club and, with enough extra payment, one can potentially own or run any kind of business. Interaction takes place via written or voice chat. The registration in Second Life is for free as are basic functions. In order to buy things in the virtual world one has to pay real money, however, i.e. the regular user just has a limited creative scope and extra goods and services have to be purchased in much the same way as in the real world. A lot of real life companies and institutions have opened up branches in Second Life, and many have already closed them again however.

There has been a big discussion about whether Second Life is dead, a stable site but just for nerds or whether it is going to be more alive than ever in the future. There is as big a debate about what to think about the use of Second Life in general, so your answers to the introductory question might also have been:

Opposing views on Second Life (SL)

- A great chance of interacting with new people
- A fantastic way of using your imagination
- A flight from reality
- A great playing field for perpetrators
- ..

We do see the very different facets of Second Life and are going to discuss the apparently huge potential for language lessons as well as the downsides and dangers here.

Being absorbed into a different world and virtually acting while talking to people who are equally absorbed into this virtual world provides us with the opportunity for authentic language use. Also, when acting in a role that is different from your normal one in situations that are different from those you are normally in, people's imagination is potentially stirred which can be a very powerful tool for learning (see Egan 2008). Just joining the English speaking Second Life community in general has been reported to have positive effects on peoples' English level but there are also a vast amount of initiatives, non-profit ventures as well as commercial ones, which aim at improving their users' English skills. There are language schools with representations in Second Life, such as *Avatar Languages*, *English Village* or *LanguageLab*, as well as initiatives for creating tandem networks, such as *Teach You, Teach Me*, within the virtual world. The British Council Hong Kong has created an island for learning English in Teen Second

Second Life's potential for learning and teaching English

Life which can be joined for free. Apart from the opportunity of interacting with others in English, there are adventures, i.e. quests, to be mastered on the island, such as the collection of the right clues in order to be able to draw Merlin's sword from the stone.

Screenshot 8.9: A scene from a LanguageLab session within SL (Taken from: http://www.languagelab.com/)

Scenarios for teaching English with Second Life

The language learning communities described above are all closed communities within the big world of Second Life, with Teen Second Life being a protected version for 13 to 17-year-olds that is supposedly free from dangerous contents and actions. Learning environments, such as those briefly sketched above, provide very different opportunities for language learning. Some of the scenarios for language learning in SL are listed in table 8.1 below.

WebQuests / Treasure hunts	Teachers and material designers can create an environment in which students, who are all logged on, look out for clues in order to solve a problem or find a hidden treasure. Depending on the level of simulation or the degree to which the Quest is organized through different tools, it will be more like a real life treasure hunt or like a regular WebQuest.

Simulations of events	Scenes that participants of a language course might want to practice, such as "an evening at a restaurant" for a business dinner or "going shopping for clothes" can be simulated in a realistic way. In the same way press conferences or panel discussions can be simulated with participants taking on pre-defined roles.
Attending "real" events	There already are events within SL that participants can take part in with their avatars. There are online headquarters of EUROCALL and CALICO, the academic organizations which discuss and promote the use of Technology in Europe and the USA respectively. There are rooms and surfaces for presentations in these headquarters, so that any kind of PowerPoint presentation, film clip or document can be displayed to viewers and through voicechat presentations and subsequent discussions can be organized in the same way as during events in real life.
Trips through virtual cities / countries	Whole cities and countries have been simulated in a quite realistic way – exploring the countries and interacting with people can help to gain quasi realistic experience. The tasks, which can again result in a kind of WebQuest, can raise awareness of cultural aspects.
Task based learning	A lot of the activities described above would not work without setting good tasks for guiding students' work. Within the virtual environment chosen for a language course, students need some inspiration for what they could do, so information or opinion gap activities set by the instructor are a good means of guiding the interaction within the environment.
Creating films for demonstration purposes	Teachers can produce films in which they model communicative situations with aims at discourse level or in which they can introduce new vocabulary and language structures. In those films the characters within the film can either be part of a communicative situation that the students are supposed to be able master or the avatar can take the role of a teacher or demonstrator.

Table 8.1: Lesson ideas for the use of SL in language lessons (adapted from Davies 2010: http://www.ict4lt.org/en/index.htm)

Even though there is a lot that SL has to offer for language learning, interaction within SL cannot be as natural as in real life, i.e. we do not have all the means for interaction, such as mime and gesture, available with such ease, we cannot see the lips of people we interact with and the sound quality still limits the audibility of individual sounds and accents of people (AVALON 2009b). Also, coming back to the comments at the beginning

Limitations to learning English with Second Life

of this chapter, we would like to emphasise that students' use of SL, also including the English version, will have to be viewed in much the same way as their use of online games and computer games in general.

As long as interacting in (Teen) SL is still seen as a pastime and is not an addiction, i.e. as long as people have the feeling that they are in control of what they are doing, the opportunity of using Second Life and also learning English in SL, can certainly be an enrichment. When the boundaries between the real and Second Life are blurred, e.g. because people spend more time in their virtual identity than in their real one, or when people start to act in a way within Second Life in which they would or should not act in their real lives, this certainly does become problematic.

Part of the fun of computer games is that people can do things that they could or would not do in their real lives. In many games the social practices are quite limited, however, and people know more or less what they sign up for when they start out with the game. In SL the range of social practices is also defined by the creators at the company Linden Lab but their range is almost as broad as in the real world. This results in a different level of responsibility for one's actions within Second life. We always have to take into consideration that through our avatars we are still interacting with real people. There have been reports of couples divorcing because of betrayal in second life and also of a teenager who worked as a prostitute in the virtual world in order to gain the currency for buying things within the virtual community. These examples illustrate once more that the virtual world of Second Life is imperfect in the very same way as our real world and also how dangerous the application is especially for young users who manage to get into the adult version of SL.

Instead of offering our own concluding remarks, i.e. instead of answering the introductory question to this sub-section ourselves, we would like to finish with more fragmentary examples of what SL possibly is or is not by providing a hopefully balanced mix of quotes :

> Jugendliche verbringen derzeit sieben Stunden mit Schlafen, gefolgt von fünfeinhalb Stunden Bildschirm-Medien-Nutzung und vier Stunden Schule (bezogen auf eine normale Sieben-Tage-Woche). Damit ist die Zeit vor dem Bildschirm der Hauptweg, Erfahrungen zu machen. Diese Erfahrungen schlagen sich im

Gehirn nieder, führen langfristig zur Ausbildung von Einstellungen, Kenntnissen und Fähigkeiten.

Wenn wir im wirklichen Leben miteinander umgehen, so gibt es bestimmte Regeln, an die wir uns halten. Diese sind kulturell tradiert und haben sich über die Jahrhunderte hin bewährt. Was ist davon zu erwarten, wenn in einer virtuellen Realität Menschen ohne Konsequenzen Kontakt haben? Man könnte sagen, dass hier über Räume und Grenzen hinweg ein Austausch möglich ist, der das gegenseitige Verständnis verbessert. Dieser optimistischen Version muss entgegen gehalten werden, dass in einer rein durch Marktgesichtspunkten beherrschten zweiten Welt sehr viele Dinge geschehen, die wir eigentlich nicht wollen: Ein Problem von SL ist mittlerweile Pornographie und ein weiteres Kriminalität. Jugendliche brauchen Kontakt zu anderen realen Menschen, nicht zu "Avataren" auf Bildschirmen. Ich glaube nicht, dass jemand tatsächlich zu einem besseren Menschen wird, wenn er sich dauernd in einer "Halbwelt" aufhält.

(Manfred Spitzer; cited on: http://www.bildung-plus.de/medien/ sites/Second_life_education.html)

It's the ultimate sandbox to build whatever you can imagine. Hospitals & universities are using it, Harvard Law School is one among many who teaches there. Reuters missed every major story while they had a site in SL. It's wonderful for builders, artists, and live performers to start out, but no-one is going to login to it to buy trainers.
Pam, UK

I spent two years on Second Life. Were it not for finding good company in the trivia game community, I would never have stayed that long. Most of the other things I found a bit pointless and superficial.
Rickson Barbosa

Don't confuse hype with success. I am sure you are as aware of Gartner's Hype Cycle as I am: Second Life has been through the over-hype, where it suffered particularly from corporates completely missing the point – they could hardly do anything but fail. Today, Second Life seems healthily on what Gartner called the Slope of Enlightenment, on the way to the Plateau of Productivity. Where Second Life really scores today in my view is as a teaching environment, and as a venue for virtual conferences and events which are far more cost-effective and environmentally sound than flying people across the world. As far as teaching environments are concerned, look at the Frideswide region where the University of Oxford's WWI Poetry Digital Archive has established a stunning presentation of aspects of their collection in a simulated Western Front.

Richard E, Cambridge UK

Second Life is boring! You can't do anything without spending money, so for the person casually checking it out, there's absolutely nothing to attract them. And despite the comment in the article about "talking to weirdos", it's actually quite difficult to find anyone in there to talk to at all.

Vince, Croydon, UK

I have been visiting Second Life on and off for three years and it is what you make of it, like anything else. I do not consider myself to be a weirdo and I am certainly not looking for cheap thrills or an extra-marital affair. I have SL friends who I regularly chat with and they range from university professors to gardeners and from teachers to artists. A wide social mix of people visit Second Life, which is certainly the best virtual world without a shadow of a doubt. As a building tool Second Life is terrific eg: I designed a kitchen extension online that you can walk around as opposed to paying an architect a fortune to draw it for me. It is not for everybody but to write it off now would be incredibly premature.

RC Robjohn, London

It's better than any social networking or chat room. It's more interactive. Although there are a lot of rude people on there especially new users/avatars. I met my wife on there. However you can grow bored of it and its speed sometimes is slow. I now go on it once every couple of weeks.

Rob H, Wolves, UK

Taken from: http://news.bbc.co.uk/2/hi/8367957.stm

8.7 More social software tools

What other tools do you know that can be used by students to be creative in lessons?

As the final point of the last section already implies, there is no real conclusion with regard to the potential of social software for languages lessons. And, as stated in the beginning of the chapter, there is no definitive list of the best tools available as there are new ones emerging constantly. The general trend is to create mashups, i.e. take features from different existing social software products and mix them in a new way. With the increasing number of technical options, the possibilities of becoming creative in software design have increased tremendously. Below we will describe just a few tools which, we think, can really be of help if we want students to be active in language lessons.

Voicethread

Voicethread is a tool that allows you to develop communication around media. This can be a picture, a film clip or any other kind of document one wants to use as a discussion point. The tool allows you to add comments by recording a clip, leaving a voice message, by writing a comment or by combining the display of a document with an audio recording and even demonstrations on screen, such as drawing a circle around numbers in a table in order to highlight aspects while you are talking.

Screenshot 8.10: a snapshot from the http://voicethread.com/ site

This tool enables students to prepare presentations that they can share with classmates or anyone online and it also enables the other members of a class to comment on each others' products. Because the tool is so flexible, it can be used at any level for any kind of content, from the discussion of a literary text to any kind of current affair, academic or business topic or personal account of experiences. As it allows for the integration of visuals to such a high extent, even low level English learners can create fairly professional products. Additionally it caters for different learner styles in that the products as well as the responses can take very different formats.

Zimmertwins

Zimmertwins.ca is a tool that helps users create their own films with cartoon characters. They can choose characters, actions for those characters, and their facial expressions. They can insert script in different ways and choose the music that should play along.

Screenshot 8.11 from http://www.zimmertwins.ca/movie/howto

Screenshot 8.12: film clip from http://www.zimmertwins.ca/node/904258

Although the options are limited by the choices of the programme, the vast amount of different combinations definitely allows for real creativity. Because of its limitations the tool is more suitable for beginner than for advanced learners.

Voki

With voki learners can create their own personal avatar and add it to their website, blog, e-mails or social networks. To get their avatar to speak, students can either record their own voice or can use the text to speech function in English, i.e. any message they type in, will be spoken by the avatar. Limits are typos and also uncommon words, such as Tabouleh, a Lebanese salad, which is actually very commonly found in Britain. Through their chosen avatar students can act and develop their virtual character in a similar way as in Second Life, only without the 3d environment around it. There are already reports of teachers who have used voki successfully in their language lessons. For an example, see a TeachersTV clip on using technology in language lessons (http://www.teachers.tv/videos/37336).

Animoto

The tool Animoto will turn raw data, such as videos clips and photos into a multimedia show with music, professional blend overs, fade ins and outs and other kinds of animations. This tool

Screenshot 8.13: voki avatars (http://www.teachers.tv/videos/37336)

can be used by beginners as well as more advanced learners, e.g. if they would like to blend different videoclips, they have produced, into one production.

Glogster

With glogster interactive posters including images, videos and music can be created easily. Again, this is a new mix of functions used in other tools already, this time with the format of a poster as a final outcome. Although this tool can potentially be used for all target groups, it will probably have the biggest appeal for children and younger teenagers.

8.8 Focus on Research

How motivated would you be to use blogs in lessons?

The variety of research on using social software for language learning is as manifold as the tools themselves and the types of interaction they allow. There has been quite a bit of research on the use of blogs in language lessons showing that blogs can indeed effectively facilitate language learning and teaching (Betts & Glogoff, 2005; Bloch, 2007). The use of blogs seems to have an especially large effect on the complexity of produced texts on grammatical correctness and fluency (Hewett 2000). One likely reason is that students will be more motivated because their text will be read by other people.

In research on the use of voice blogs Sun (2009) has found distinct stages in the learners' output. They all seemed to have gone through the stages of conceptualizing, brainstorming, articulation, monitoring, and evaluating, i.e. they by no means causally recorded messages but went through similar planning and editing stages as are known for writing texts. Apparently, the students' attitudes were especially positive at the beginning – in later stages the interest wore off. Students seemed on the whole to have wished for a bigger audience. What Sun's research has in common with prior research is that she found the same kind of care in students' work as the other researchers which could be due to the fact that the students' work is more public than regular course work. There are questions that remain to be answered, however. For example how far was the students' behaviour in this study culture specific? Also, what kind of task set up is needed in order to maintain the students' enthusiasm?

Another huge research project that is worth mentioning here is AVALON. The EU funded the AVALON Project, which stands for Access to Virtual and Action Learning Live Online, and aims at creating and evaluating a low cost virtual learning environment within SL. It is a very comprehensive study that is coordinated by the School of Education at the University of Manchester and is carried out in cooperation with many different partners, mostly universities, across Europe (see avalon-project.ning.com/). The project includes expert surveys, expert interviews as well as pre- and post-course surveys. Several courses with different target groups were monitored, such as a Business English Course, a teacher training course or an Italian Beginners course.

Some of the results that are reported in the three AVALON evaluation reports (2009a, 2009b, 2010) show that there is a big potential for language learning in SL as people can do things in SL that they could not do in real life, e.g. teleporting to different places, such as New York or London, and then meeting at a restaurant or a shopping centre somewhere completely different. Many different situations can be simulated in a 3D world that cannot as easily be simulated in any other classroom.

The results of the post-course survey showed that the participants who sent back the survey (it was voluntary) had quite a positive attitude towards the learning environment and the instructors. They rated the interaction with the instructor and in their groups within the sessions as the most important factors for success. The vast majority did not feel as though they were talking to the computer while being on the course and while knowing the real person behind the other participants' avatars was not that important for the students, knowing the real person behind the teacher's avatars was (AVALON 2010).

On the other hand the results from the expert interviews also say that SL should not be the only "place" where people set out to learn a foreign language as it cannot be a substitute for real interaction. One of the reasons is that we cannot see each others' facial expressions and the sound quality is not as good in second life, i.e. a focus on pronunciation or different accents and dialects, for example, seems difficult (AVALON 2009b:5). While the missing mime and gestures did not seem to be a big problem for the participants of the courses, they did not feel that it was easier for them to speak in the virtual environment than it is in real life. This had been one of the assumptions of the AVALON supporters.

The AVALON report also states that there are still technical problems if too many people are in SL (AVALON 2009b: 8) and also that it is a lot more difficult for SL teachers to know whether the course participants are concentrating as there is no eye contact with the real person (AVALON 2009b: 21). Interestingly enough the latter aspect did not seem to be problematic for students, the technical aspect was however. The majority of students reported that it was annoying to encounter frequent technical problems while being on the course and stated that there were more technical problems than there are in face-to-face courses (AVALON 2010). As teaching a language SL is still seen as a business model and is also regarded as an interesting non profit option by many educators at the time of writing, a lot more research in the field is to be expected in the future.

Social software is not normally made for the classroom but to help people interact outside the classroom. It will thus hopefully support the development of skills that are of relevance for life in general. There needs to be a lot more research on what kinds of skills are actually developed when using those different tools, however, and also on how the use of the tools can be optimized for the development of important language and life skills.

8.9 Classroom Ideas

How could you use a blog in order to prepare your class for an exchange programme?

Throughout the chapter it has already become clear that social software tools are designed to enable people to be creative and communicate with each other and this is also what they can be used for in English lessons. Also, it is almost impossible to describe the tools without hinting at their potential use within lessons, i.e. you will hopefully have gotten many ideas for using social software in the classrooms while reading the chapter. In this section we would like to present another idea that can be realized through the use of a blog in more detail. It is an idea that has been developed by a student group at the University of Duisburg-Essen in a seminar on using technology in English lessons.

They developed a blog that can be used to describe the interesting spots in the students' home town, in this case in Essen. The blog was only used within our course at university but was created to be used in an English class at school, prior to an exchange class arriving in the area. Students in the class are to agree on their favourite spots in their town/city in class, distribute the responsibility within the group, do research on the allocated spot, e.g. through browsing the sight's official webpage, and then to present it in the blog in their own words as it can be seen in screenshot 8.14. The partner class can then use the blog for planning their trip, can comment on the entries and in this way start a conversation with the partner class.

In a project like this students and the teacher can together decide on what the outcome should look like. There is freedom for the students as to what to present (at least they are able to negotiate the contents with the teacher) and they know that their work will not only have an audience but will potentially also be of use to their partner class as well as their own class as they are negotiating plans with each other. So students will be aware of the fact that they are writing for an audience, they see a purpose for their writing and thus there is a bigger likelihood that they will write with care, even though, in this case, they will be tempted to write in a more informal style which will also suit the purpose.

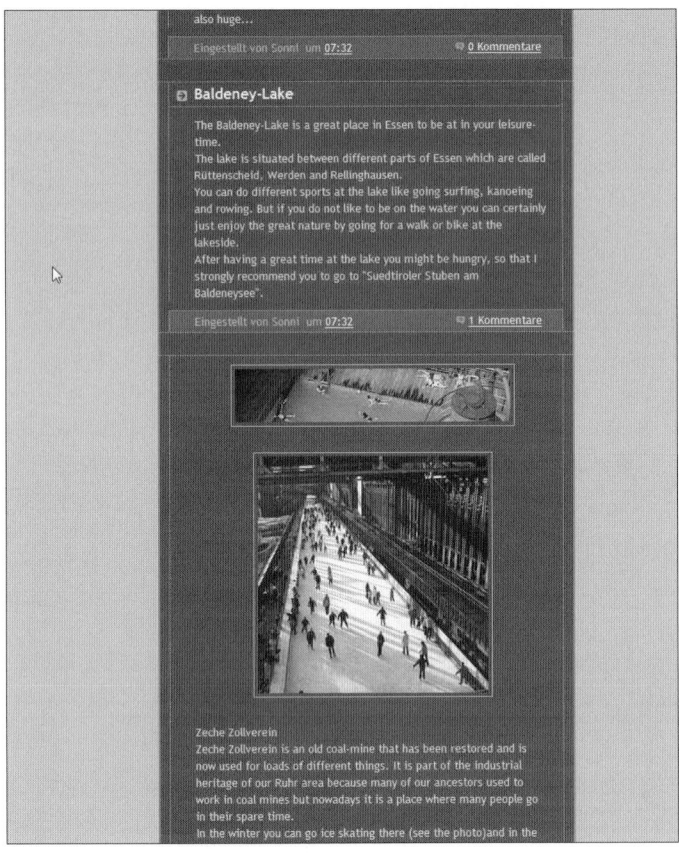

Screenshot 8.14: A University Duisburg-Essen blog on hotspots in Essen created by Sonja Krasowski and Philipp Christ (taken from: hotspot-essen.blogspot.com)

Taking the dialogic nature of blogs into account, they will expect comments from their partner class. During the project special care will have to be given to netiquette, i.e. the issue of what kinds of entries are acceptable and helpful, in order to create a positive atmosphere right from the start. If this can be maintained, one can expect the students to develop a sense of ownership for what they have planned and a sense of responsibility during the exchange as well.

Tasks

1. Which buzz words connected with social software/media use in general have been created since this book has been written? Do they indicate another change in the web?
2. How can you use wikis in your language classroom? Come up with three teaching ideas. Also list aspects to consider when using a wiki in the ways you have imagined.
3. What are the differences between a wiki and a blog? Decide for which of the desired outcomes named in the table below you would prefer using blogs and for which wikis would make more sense. Give short reasons for your choices.

	Wiki	Blog
Your own personal site		
An open source database for texts on a specific topic		
A collaboratively created website in English about your home town		
A site that informs and provides news on a given topic		
Your entry:		

4. Look at the article on the suicide due to cyberbullying in chapter 8.4. Note down how you as an English teacher can help prevent cyber bullying in your class.
5. What makes a podcast a podcast? Note down the different uses of podcast for the language classroom that have been discussed in this book so far.
6. Using the quotations on SL in chapter 8.6, write your own comment on what SL is for you.
7. Look at table 8.1 and come up with at least three concrete tasks for language lessons in SL. If you have no prior experience with SL, watch any demo clip online to get inspiration.

SO WHAT? | 9

9.1 Value added: Developing Intercultural Agency

Think of everything you have read about in this book so far and try to summarize in one sentence what value is added by using computers in English lessons before you read on.

We would agree that lessons with computers are not per se better than lessons without computers – is it, as with all media, about the kind of use and about the aims for which they are used. Our ideas on how computers can enrich English lessons will have become clear in chapters 2 to 8 already. This chapter is going to synthesise our findings. It is also setting out to highlight what we see as our main aim in English lessons and why it might be easier to achieve with computers as facilitating tools. From our point of view this main aim of English lessons is to develop something that we call Intercultural Agency.

Agency as the aim of language teaching

Agency, defined by Janet Murray (1997:126) as "the satisfying power to take meaningful action and see the results of our decisions and choices", can be seen as one of the main aims of modern language teaching as it entails the aim of empowering, enabling learners and groups of learners to achieve whatever they want to achieve (see also Warschauer 2004, Rüschoff 2009, van Lier 2010). As an aim for language teaching it means that we enable learners to achieve their aims by using the foreign language. It is a can-do approach that goes along with a higher focus on developing skills in English lessons, rather than mainly developing the knowledge of, for example, grammar and vocabulary. For Agency in the real world these skills will need to be developed in holistic situations that require complex decision making and real time interactions. E.g., if we assume that the situations in the photos below are all international situations, they all require various and complex decisions and actions that involve the use of a foreign language.

Now, the question is how to prepare students for these kinds of situations in their future lives. Despite the many years that students attend English lessons at school it won't be possible to model all the kinds of situations students might find themselves in the future. We need to identify key elements that enable students to master many different situations and that will help them to develop their Agency further without the help of teachers.

The goal of Intercultural Agency

The figure below shows our idea of what constitutes Agency, of how Agency develops and also how agents are always part of a social environment. The intercultural agent who is represented by a circle that is set within the social (and also physical) world, develops his or her Agency through interaction. Some of the interaction that leads to Agency will nowadays take place through the use of the computer, be it through online communication with others, through the cooperation when developing an online text, or through creating online documents that others will look at, to name just a few options. The benefit of interacting in English lessons with the help of the computer is that there are many opportunities for interaction between people that would not be available with such ease without the applications mentioned above.

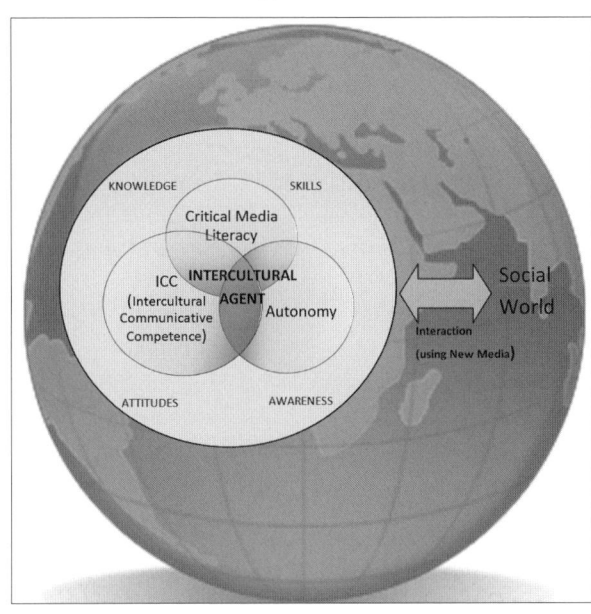

Picture 9.1: Developing Intercultural Agency in the Social World

If you consider the photos in chapter 9.1 again it is clear that you will never be able to fully describe what it takes to master those situations successfully as they are so dynamic and multifaceted that any kind of advice is bound to be incomplete. This is also, for example, often the problem of advice that novices get from experienced people. The experts might tell the novice what they do and what they think is important in certain situations but they might not even be aware of some other important elements that contribute to their success. So we think the key to sustained Agency are clusters of skills, of different kinds of knowledge, an attitude that will help to work constructively within those situations and also a considerable level of awareness. This will help us to make conscious and not only intuitive decisions and to share our experience with others. The capacities described above are developed within one's own culture and in the interaction with people from other cultures.

Although we would argue that real life intercultural situations are too complex to be encompassed in a model for Intercultural Agency, and hence have added the general categories of knowledge, skills, attitudes and awareness to the figure above, we are still convinced that there are certain clusters of those capacities that will help us in many different situations and that will thus contribute to us being a successful agent in the modern world. The three concepts to which we attribute the biggest importance are Intercultural Communicative Competence (ICC), Autonomy and (Digital) Media Literacy. Those concepts are shown as overlapping clusters as, in our view, they do share important features.

9.2 Developing Intercultural Communicative Competence (ICC)

How important is ICC in our world today?

ICC as central aim and part of Agency

The development of Intercultural Communicative Competence ICC (Byram 1997) is one of the central aims of foreign language teaching (see Müller-Hartmann & Schocker-von Ditfurth 2004, Legutke et al. 2009). It is "a person's ability to relate to and communicate with people who speak a different language and live in a different cultural context" (Byram 1997:1) and consists, according to Byram's model, of five different so-called *savoirs* which can be translated into *knowledge*, *attitudes*, *awareness*, the *skill of interpreting and relating* and the *skill of discovering and interacting* (1997: 34).

	Skills interpret and relate (*savoir comprendre*)	
Knowledge Of self and other; Of interaction: Individual and societal (*savoirs*)	Education political education critical cultural awareness (savoir s'engager)	Attitudes Relativising self Valuing other (*savoir être*)
	Skills Discover and/or interact (*savoir apprendre/faire*)	

Picture 9.2: The Byram model of Intercultural Communicative Competence

Thus, in order to be able to develop ICC one needs to gain knowledge about oneself and one's own culture and language as well as about the other respective cultures and languages. It is also important to be willing to distance oneself from one's own culture and to accept the values and attitudes of other cultures. The most important skills for the development of ICC are the skill of interpreting and relating and of discovering and interacting. The skill of interpreting and relating is essential, for example, when it comes to understanding and analyzing texts from a different culture. Here we have to interpret messages regarding the ideas and values that are communicated and relate them to our own ones. The skill of discovering and interacting is crucial in real life interactions. We have to be able to discover aspects from the other culture, have to judge what kind of action might be appropriate in the given situation and have to act in real time. At an educational level the aim is to develop critical cultural awareness regarding one's own but also other cultures, i.e. the aim is not to become a close enough copy of, for example, an English person but to become a person who is able to mediate between different cultures. In Byram's view developing ICC means turning from a tourist who might just be after the pleasures of the country into a sojourner, i.e. a guest (1997:1).

Developing ICC with the help of the computer

Instinctively one might say that just being immersed in the culture and language might do the job of developing ICC best but being dropped in at the deep end without reflection and background information might also have quite the reverse effect of strengthening stereotypes and of developing attitudes that are not helpful for further development of intercultural relations and ICC. English lessons can contribute to the development of ICC by providing opportunities for engaging with the target culture as well as one's own, by providing tasks and materials that lend themselves to discovery and discussion of crucial cultural features and by providing the opportunity for authentic interaction. Some examples of how the use of computers in lessons can help develop the different *savoirs* and how it can prepare for and also provide those real encounters in the target culture can be seen in the table below.

Savoir	Sample CALL Activities
Knowledge	– Using online portals, such as bbc.co.uk or the sites of online newspapers to gather background information – WebQuests on a given topic – Consulting an online encyclopedia (e.g. Wikipedia)
Skill of interpreting and relating	– E-mail projects (asynchronous, gives time for interpreting and relating) – Watching/showing film clips on topic (e.g. from YouTube or a news portal) – Working with texts from the web (newspaper articles, poems, lyrics) – Interacting through blogs or wikis on a topic of interest (a film, such as Slumdog Millonaire or a novel, such as The Kite Runner)
Skill of discovering and interacting	– Skype project (interacting in real time, if wanted with videoconferencing) – Using Second Life (but with care – see comment later on in the chapter) – Training one's language skills with the help of tutorial software

Attitudes	– E-mail projects (including reflection) – Viewing video podcasts, e.g. film clips from *East is East* etc. – WebQuest on a given topic, such as *Australia* or *The UN and peace keeping* – Creating blogs or wikis on a topic of interest (a film, such as *Slumdog Millonaire* or a novel, such as *The Kite Runner*)
Critical Cultural awareness	– WebQuest on a given topic, such as *Health Care in the USA vs. in Germany* – E-mail (Cultura) projects including reflections on values and attitudes

Table 9.1: Supporting the savoirs through technology use

People who have developed a high degree of competence in all *savoirs* are more likely to be successful agents in situations in which they have to be spontaneous, i.e. in which they have to display the skill of discovery and interaction, as they can draw on all their *savoirs* when acting. The use of the computer can potentially add value to English lessons in the attempt to develop ICC as it facilitates interaction with people from the target cultures, it makes authentic and up to date materials available at an instant and enables learners to share their results with others quickly.

The Iceberg model of culture illustrates how difficult it is to discover and become aware of many aspects of a culture however. It shows that only a very small part of it is visible to the eye and that most cultural aspects might not even be part of the conscious knowledge of the members of the respective culture. A lot of beliefs, values and feelings only become conscious when a conflict arises and when alternative values are considered and discussed.

Picture 9.2: The Iceberg Model of Culture (Taken from: http://www.international.gc.ca/cfsi-icse/cil-cai/maga-zine/vo2no1/doc3-eng.pdf)

In language lessons this is where literary texts and films as well as projects including online communication have their place, partly because they can provide access to the thoughts and feelings of others and can help us to become aware of what we think and feel. The cultura model of e-mail exchanges (see chapter 2.3) focuses on making some of those hidden aspects of culture visible and does thus try to contribute to the development of ICC in learners.

9.3 Developing Autonomy

How autonomous are you as a learner? What does the term mean for you?

Fostering learners' autonomy

The way in which the computer as a tool or even as a tutor makes resources a lot more available to learners and makes interaction with others a lot easier, also facilitates the development of independence in learners. This is important for helping learners to become autonomous which is or should in our view be another aim of modern language teaching. Autonomy is a bit of a fuzzy term that has been defined in many different ways, with some of the definitions coming close to the idea of Agency described in this chapter (see van Lier 2010). In this publication we are referring to Henri Holec's definition of autonomy as "the ability to take charge of one's own learning" (Holec 1981:3). It is important to say in this context that autonomous individuals are always seen as members of social groups, i.e. the ideal state is not to produce autistic individuals. We assume Vygotsky's sociocultural approach in this book, with the idea that new knowledge is primarily learned in interaction with the social environment and is gradually integrated into the individual's knowledge and belief system (Vygotsky 1973). This also means that we do assume that collaboration with others and finding one's own role in groups are vital parts of the learning process. From a political point of view, the ideal state would not be anarchy with many individuals fighting for their rights but a democracy with respectful relationships and shared power.

In a lot of institutional contexts the concept of autonomy is restricted to self-instructed learning or to the expectations that learners should be able to organize their learning in such a way that they can achieve the set goals independently. The broader concept comprises the idea of emancipating learners however. To some extent it also assumes that learners will naturally learn autonomously once they are really motivated. As we meet learners with different biographies of learning at school, we will not always find this intrinsic motivation in all students straight away. Helping learners to become autonomous is the teacher's responsibility then (Dam 2003). This can be done through providing inspiring tasks and by gradually giving learners more responsibility for their learning process and also more freedom. Once learners have a say in what is done in the classroom, can be creative and work towards a goal that they identify with, they are more likely to develop intrinsic motivation. The teacher can help create and sustain this motivation through so-called *scaffolding*, i.e. providing a scaffold for the learners that helps them to succeed when working on a task and that finally helps them to progress to a higher level (Wood, Bruner & Ross 1976). Different types and features of *scaffolding* have been described by Donato (1994). The table below shows those different features and examples of how the use of computer applications can already serve as a scaffold.

Computer applications as scaffolds

1) recruiting interest in the task	— Using authentic materials, such as film clips, from the web or designing an attractive WebQuest or blog to be filled with contents can already stir up interest that has to be maintained through setting appropriate tasks
2) simplifying the task	— Research on the web can be simplified through the use of a WebQuest — The structures that are given in Social Software do provide guidance already. Those programmes have been designed in order to simplify the task of creating an online document, so that as many people as possible can contribute, i.e. this is a scaffold that teachers can make use of in their lessons
maintaining the pursuit of the goal	— structured tasks within a WebQuest can help maintain the pursuit of the goal

	– Using presentation software can help students structure the output, keep pursuing their task and makes the results more professional. – Using a word processor instead of producing a handwritten text provides a spell check and a thesaurus, for example, and also makes the process of editing more effective and less painful than if done in handwriting
marking critical features and discrepancies between what has been produced and the ideal solution	– the tutor function in educational software can give feedback on the success in very structured exercises and tasks – can be done by the students themselves (and their peers) by looking at model versions (e.g. of a business letter) on the internet or in a tutorial programme
controlling frustration during problem solving	– the user friendly structure of a lot of web 2.0 applications help to minimize frustration during problem solving

Table 9.2: Scaffolding through the use of computer applications

These are just some examples of how the use of the use of the computer can potentially support students' inspiration and persistence. There is still a lot of scaffolding to be done by the teacher, however, as students will still have to accomplish the tasks even though the computer might make some things easier. Also, all the interactional processes within the classrooms and within groups will, of course, be as much of an issue as it would be in lessons without computers. One of the goals of all the endeavours in English lessons is to support students in their autonomy of language use. The final aim in languages lessons is from our point of view, however, to foster students' motivational autonomy (Ushioda 1996, 2003), i.e. the capacity of continuously motivating themselves to keep pursuing the goals they have set for themselves. This can best be done if students are gradually enabled to work independently on projects, similar to the ones described in this book, that require persistency and the ability to structure the processes within the project but that also give students freedom of choice and responsibility for process and outcome. In this way teachers can help students to keep developing Agency throughout their lives, i.e. autonomy can be seen as an important prerequisite for lifelong learning and for sustained Agency in the modern world.

9.4 Developing Critical Media Literacy

How reflective are you in your media use? Would you regard yourself rather as someone who consumes or as someone who tends to create things?

Another aspect of vital importance for sustained Agency is, from our point of view, critical media literacy. The aim of developing media literacy is a traditional aim of teaching in general, i.e. understanding principles of how communication and manipulation through media works, how to make use of them most effectively and even how to create them has also had its place in curricula for English language teaching in Germany for decades. What has changed over the times is that it is not primarily about shaping analytical and academic skills any more. It is increasingly also about enabling students to use those tools that are of importance outside educational and academic contexts. On the one hand these are the tools that they might need to use in their jobs later on, i.e. the skill of being able to use word processors, presentation software or e-mailing software is something that will be taken for granted in most jobs. As almost no letters are hand written anymore, writing letters or e-mails on the computer means that English lessons are taking account of the common social practices that we want to prepare our students for.

On the other hand enabling students to use those media they use at home wisely is becoming more important as media use of children and teenagers has increased tremendously throughout the last few decades. Understanding the "grammar", i.e. the underlying structures and functions, of these applications and the roles they can play in peoples' lives, will help students to stay critical agents rather than being easy prey for any kind of manipulation.

In the majority of computer applications the social practices are crucial, i.e. it is important in which social context, how and for what purposes they are used (see Cutrim Schmid 2009). This means that computer applications are neither inherently good or

Critical Media Literacy

Critical Theory of Technology

bad, it is their use that we have to shape and watch as teachers. This idea is part of the so called critical theory of technology that can be contrasted with a deterministic and also with an instrumental view of technology:

- In the instrumental view technology is just seen as a tool that is neutral and can be used of for any aim. No influences of the tool on the individual or society are assumed.
- Determinism assumes that the existance of certain kinds of technology will cause certain results in itself. These results can be good or bad: either technology is seen as something overtly positive that can solve problems and can thus improve situations which are less than ideal (e.g. "Computers are the ideal tool for learning – in the future we won't need books any more") or the technological applications themselves are seen as the source of a problem either for the individual or society (e.g. "Computers destroy our children's creativity").

In a critical theory technology is neither seen as completely neutral nor is it seen as a force in itself. It is not neutral because technology is historically embedded and is created in a specific social context (Cutrim Schmid 2009). Thus, the structures will be influenced by the ideas and beliefs of those who create them. Control over the structure and the accessibility will be done by those who have the power to do so. Also, to assume that, for example, the availability of cars, the emergence of the PC and now of social software have not affected individuals' behaviour as much as society would certainly be naive. Our social contexts are influenced by these developments and education is slowly being influenced as well. Within those social contexts there is usually ample scope for different social practices while using the respective applications, however, even though the applications' structures limit the options of how they can be used.

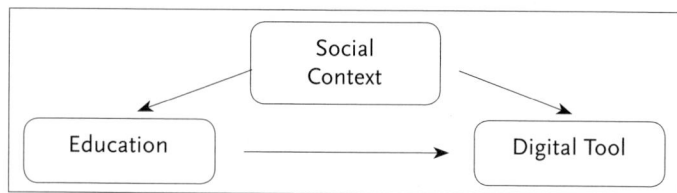

Picture 9.3: The interplay between social context, education and (digital) tools

For an example of how different social practices can influence the nature of the tool, we take a look at alternative uses of social networking sites. Networking sites, such as Facebook or Myspace, can, for example, be used as platforms for meeting new people and for keeping in touch with people you know. Depending on what kind of contact you would be interested in, you could, for example, join interest groups (which is common practice in studiVZ), you could build up a fairly private network by browsing the respective contacts of your contacts or you could just open up your whole profile to everyone in order to see who might be attracted by it and possibly browse the net for people who do the same. Needless to say the last option might seem like the most surprising one at first sight but also is potentially the most hazardous one. Enthusing students about useful and enjoyable options will increase their Agency and will often be more effective than shere warnings. There should be limits as to what we want to enthuse our students about however. So even though there are studies suggesting that the use of the English versions of the game *World of Warcraft* has a positive effect on learners' language proficiency (Bryant 2006; Nardi, Ly & Harris 2007) as the users are constantly communicating about contents they are interested in in the foreign language, we do have, to say the least, mixed feelings about suggesting the use of these kinds applications to students. Suggesting that students should engage in strategic planning and virtual conduct of war seems questionable and due to the range of social practices they encourage, we fail to see their role in an educational context. The computer use that we would like to encourage and support is one that helps students achieve the aims that they set in their real lives and one that either involves or facilitates direct contact with the real social world.

Tasks

1. Reflect on the term Agency by analyzing a day that you have spent in an English speaking country. Take notes on how your Agency got you through the day. What might have been lacking? Could any lessons have prepared you for that? How?
2. Try to list what mastering the situations depicted in the photos in chapter 9.1 requires.

3. International conference calls are common practice in international companies. Think of possibilities for enabling your students to take part in a conference call. Is the computer of any help there?

4. The aim of developing ICC is that students reach a so-called third space (Kramsch 1993), i.e. a space that is remote not only from one's own culture but also from the target culture. Referring back to this chapter as well as to chapter 2.3 think of a design for an e-mail project that might help develop this capacity.

5. Go to http://australiaquest.wordpress.com/ and list the ways in which the WebQuest provides scaffolding for gaining information on a given topic. To what extent are the students really autonomous when they work through such a WebQuest?

6. Make a list of five computer applications students (should) know nowadays. Then also list what they need to know, be aware of and be able to do in order to be critical media literates.

Computer Application	Knowledge	Skills	Awareness

...

7. Supporting students' Agency in English lessons is highly demanding for the school and the teacher. Write down five postulations for changes that are necessary in order to be able to fulfil this task.

TEACHING ENGLISH WITH COMPUTERS: | 10
WHAT'S NEXT?

Where do you think all the technological trends will lead us? And where do they lead education in schools? Close your eyes and try to imagine what learning will be like in about twenty years' time.

I bet your vision of technological developments will be many-faceted. The different atmospheres in the scenes that you have created in your mind will possibly range from the idea of slick and elegant technological devices being integrated into our lives to quite pessimistic scenes like in movies, such as *The Matrix* or *2001*. Maybe your mind went blank because with the pace of technological development at the moment it is even hard to guess what the technological devices in a couple of years' time will look like.

We would like to take care that we neither paint a too colourful picture of the future in this chapter, nor an overtly grey or black one here, i.e. we will not go for any kind of deterministic view. Again, we take a fairly critical and reflective position, by also considering the challenges we will have to meet in schools in the future in order to be able to make use of the potential technology for English lessons that support Intercultural Agency and we will only make tentative attempts to predict future developments in the use of technology in society and in education.

10.1 Current Challenges

Think back to the classroom ideas presented in this book. Do you see any challenges in putting those into practice in the schools you know?

Equipment in schools

There certainly are challenges to be met and some of you might think that the classroom ideas described in this book are all very nice but not easy to put into practice at school. Technological equipment in schools seems to be one issue that presents a practical constraint for many ideas that require, for example, the use of an electronic whiteboard or the use of many computers at the same time. Most of the data is anecdotal, i.e. taken from students' reactions in seminars who often claim that in the schools they have visited lately, this or that kind of computer use would certainly not be possible due to a lack of equipment. The latest figures on equipment in schools in Germany from the year 2006 (Bundesministerium für Bildung und Forschung 2006) do not paint such a black picture. In primary school, on the whole, 12 children share one computer, at secondary level the number rises to 1 computer for 11 students. In primary school about half of the computers were in the classrooms, half of them in computer suites. In secondary schools 62 % of the desktop computers were in suites, with only 32 % being installed in classrooms (2006: 6). While it would be ideal to have a higher number of computers available in classrooms, especially for a casual integration of computers into every day teaching, having computer suites that classes then use alternately, is at least a good enough starting point.

In the year 2006 89% of all secondary schools possessed a digital projector (2006: 15) that, together with a laptop, could be used for those teaching ideas that allow for the computer to be used as a projection device or as a resource in the corner of the classroom. For enabling group and project work with computers, mobile solutions, such as a set of laptops and a wireless LAN network rather than a whole networked computer room, might be the most practical option. In this way many projects described in this book can already be put into practice. In the future we might also be able to rely on students' multimedia phones as devices in lessons but so far this is only an option in some schools. On the whole we have to hope that falling prices will make technology available for schools on a larger scale and also that schools will be able to spend more money on equipment, so that the gap in standards of equipment between German schools and schools in many other countries in Europe, e.g. the UK, can be closed. Another hope is that we will find an effective way of helping schools to keep the new computer systems running.

Some teachers might see the use of some of the applications described for their lessons but might fear the challenge of fitting time consuming projects into their regular teaching time. Although we believe projects to be more efficient in many ways than more teacher centred lessons that try to convey contents in a more condensed period of time, we do acknowledge that learning in projects does take time and do see the time pressure that some of the educational trends, such as a shortened time for secondary

Curricular challenges

schooling (e.g. *G8*) and more centralized exams bring with them. It will always be possible to take small steps, however, so it seems advisable and feasible to start by incorporating authentic tasks into English lessons (see Müller-Hartmann & Schocker-von Ditfurth 2004) and work with fairly structured projects that allow the teacher to guide and monitor the learning process easily before daring to completely open up lessons.

Teachers' levels of
Intercultural Agency

In order to be able to make use of the full potential of computers for language lessons, teachers need to be intercultural agents with a high level of autonomy, ICC and critical media literacy themselves. Obviously teachers will show varying degrees of proficiency in different domains. Teacher education will have to support the development of these domains by raising future teachers' awareness of their strengths and provide them with the means to improve their own Agency throughout their career. One way of supporting future teachers is by giving them the opportunity of experiencing the same type of teaching that they hope to be able to use in class later on. Finally, even teachers with a high degree of critical media literacy might find it challenging to keep up with the pace of technological developments that influence their students' lives and can potentially have a positive impact on their English lessons.

10.2 Technological Trends in Society

Instead of imagining a scene way ahead in time, just think about current trends in technological development and about new social practices that are emerging with them.

It feels daring to try to predict what will happen in the near future in a book as a lot of the developments we foresee now might already be outdated or might never have taken place by the time you are reading this. Warschauer's prediction on the future of CALL from the year 2004 was fairly accurate but within three years all the developments had already taken place and some of them, especially the more technical ones, almost seemed like old hat.

Warschauer (2004: 3) predicted, for example, a development from cable connections to wireless connections, a move from dial-up to permanent, direct connections, from narrowband to broadband connections and also from the use of personal computers to the use of portable devices. All these predictions have, as has already been said, become true within very few years after Warschauer had published his article. So you might want to excuse us if we, in this book, decide stick to describing current trends and only have a very tentative look into the future.

One very visible trend that reflects Warschauer's predictions is that throughout the last few decades technological devices have become faster, more mobile and more invisible. The technical possibilities have gone so far that it is not even user friendly anymore to make technological devices as small and as light as possible as we still have to be able to handle those devices and we also would like to feel that we have something valuable in our hands. This has lead to the effect that some devices are even made heavier through additional weights, so that they do not seem too light to us.

Integration of functions

More and more functions have been integrated into one device. New browser technologies start to blur the line between functions belonging to operating systems and those typical functions of browsers. These enable users to operate all sorts of applications wherever they are and to store great amounts of information online. This constant availability of computer applications and the resulting growth in flexibility have led to a more casual integration of communicating through the internet and gaining information from the web into all kinds of real life situations. Since mobile phones have turned into multimedia devices, that are now also referred to as handheld devices, Personal Digital Assistants (PDA) or smart phones due to the multiple functions they fulfil, no one necessarily needs to sit down at a desk and switch on a computer for virtual communication or for finding the best route to a chosen place anymore. Mobile phones are cameras and radios, MP3 players, audio recorders, games machines, audio-and videoconferencing devices, calculators, data storage devices, navigators and much more.

Those devices can provide information on demand, be it about the weather, train times, news about topics of interest or new friends entries on Facebook. With the abundance of apps available comes the need to personalize our virtual environments by choosing what aspects we want to make most frequent use of and what kind information we are most interested in (see Godwin-Jones 2009).

Personalized virtual environments

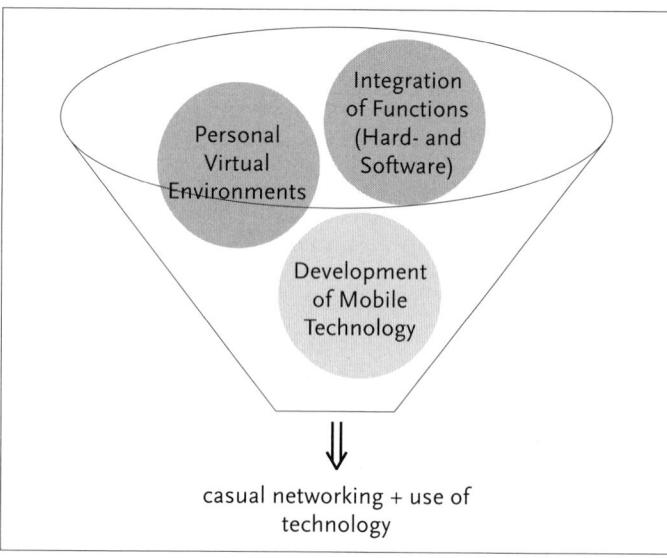

Picture 10.1: Networking and use of technology

Casual use of technology
We arrived at what van Dijk calls the stage of a network society long ago (van Dijk 1991).

The intensity with which people engage in virtual networks still differs tremendously however. At the time of writing, phones that integrate all kinds of different apps are still new and expensive. We don't doubt that they will be accepted as normal by the time you read this chapter. There will still be people in the future, however, who spend several hours per day engaging in social networking through the internet and also people who only sporadically engage in virtual networks. Through mobile technology this networking is on the whole becoming more and more casual and spread throughout the day and does not necessarily take place at a certain period of time in the day which people have allocated to keeping in contact via social network or e-mail.

The semantic web
On the web there are an increasing number of attempts to provide users with more useful information and suggestions than they actually set out to seek in the first place. If you choose a book online you will see suggestions on the page about other books you might be interested in. So far this mostly only works within one site. The vision of internet creator Tim Berners-Lee and the

w3 consortium at the MIT in Massachusetts is to get this effect across sites. His aim is to standardize the formats and the language used on the web and to open up the underlying data files to such an extent that programmes will be able to link contents of websites in a meaningful way. In this way the current web would turn into a so-called semantic web.

There have been attempts to make use of the existing web to link contents in a meaningful way through mash-up sites like tripit.com. If you send your travel documents to the site it will try to extract and store the most important information. A schedule is created automatically that is also available on the traveller's mobile phone and is connected with information on any travel delays and with additional useful information, such as the weather. Berners-Lee's hope for the future is to make these kinds of services more effective and information more accessible by, for example, using the same kinds of codes for all sites.

10.3 Technology in Education

Considering challenges for schools as well as technological trends, what do you think technology use in education in Germany will look like in the near future?

We have seen in the past that it is taking a lot of time for technology to be established in mainstream education. So far a lot of technology use takes place due to the personal commitment of individual teachers and the normal situation in schools ranges from basically no technology use at all to the whole organization of course work taking place through, for example, a blog or other online tools with a natural integration of technological tools into teaching and learning. In 2006 a considerable number of 58% of primary schools indicated that they use the computer in languages lessons either often or occasionally, in secondary schools the number was even higher, with 77% of the schools claiming that they use computers in language lessons either often or occasionally. If you only look at schools which stated they often use computer in languages lessons, the number decreases tremendously, to 16% in the primary school and 25% at secondary level.

"Normality" in schools

Among those schools that make frequent use of the computer, there are initiatives and projects that involve laptops or even smart phones for the whole class which then enable teachers and students to communicate frequently, send voice mails or other files to each other and to use the phone for any kind of media reception or production. On the whole 2% of all schools in Germany had laptop classes in the year 2006 (Bundesministerium für Bildung und Forschung 2006: 12), with no reference being made to smartphone classes as yet as those devices only became readily available and affordable later.

Normalization of technology use

One reason for this difference in the use of technology is that school staff belong to different generations. Some teachers have just about got used to CD and DVD players while others have grown up with the multimedia PC. More teachers in the future will belong to the latter group and this will hopefully lead to technology becoming a normal part of school life as we have already hinted at in Chapter 1 (Bax 2003). This normalization will take place if future teachers have the chance during training to learn about the potential that the computer applications they already know from their private lives have for English lessons, i.e. if technology use and methodological considerations are also a natural part of teacher training programmes in the tertiary sector.

Sustainable use of technology

We would also like to utter a wish rather than describe a current trend. There is a big need for concepts for a sustainable use of technology in schools in the future, i.e. a concept that includes the frequent availability of support and updates. The need for help in order to keep computer systems running will not necessarily cease with teachers becoming digital natives as today's digital natives are increasingly rather users of computer applications than computer experts on the whole. In some countries it is normal practice to employ computer administration staff in schools. Similar concepts will probably be needed in German schools if the majority of teachers are to trust the availability of technology in their lessons.

Personal Learning Environments

The trend of providing virtual environments and integrating all sorts of different functions, as in iGoogle, in Pageflakes (see chapter 8.3) or increasingly with mobile phones, also provides us with the possibility of creating Personal Learning Environments (see Godwin-Jones 2009) for ourselves that give us instant access to the applications that we use most, e.g. dictionaries, thesauri, international social networks, news sites or whole online language courses. This is a step towards autonomous learning. Into these individualized environments we could integrate course blogs, our Skype account or links to other social networking sites that might be used for communicating and organizing work.

Students might want to and should possibly also be encouraged to keep their private networking sites private. For joint work as a class or course community social networking sites which are designed for building up interest related groups, such as Ning or Elgg, might be quite useful. There is currently is a race by the competing software companies to provide all encompassing sites that would allow individuals and interest groups to organize all their computer work solely through this individual site. As long as there is competition this will hopefully not be achieved by one single company but different people will still opt for different providers for their personalized virtual environment. Consequently, in order to be able to connect all these different people, there will still be the need for an integration of different additional applications into one's own chosen personal environment.

Again, the online world changes quickly as do the subsequent options for English teachers, so you might already know many applications that we would not have dreamt of at the time of writing. The question is, however, how quick schools are or can be to incorporate these new developments. Individual teachers can always add in new ideas to their courses. If a school decides to control the number and types of applications to be used, this is a completely different story however. For safety reasons schools will often opt for more controlled and approved environments. This is why many schools that plan to work with technology regularly use established Learning Management Systems (LMS) (see chapter 6.4) rather than any kind of newer open source application that is also accessible for the general public. So the challenge for the existing Learning Management Systems, such as Moodle or Blackboard, is to keep up with the technological developments and to allow for the integration of different kinds of applications into the fairly secure environment.

The trend of increasingly using mobile devices rather than desktop computers for web research has already influenced learning in that students can, for example, look up words online in online dictionaries and thesauri in lessons and at home. The idea

Flexibility of Learning Management Systems

of learning with mobile devices is not new – it is the increasing availability and the integration of numerous functions that open up new options. For language learning with mobile devices, such as MP3 players or smart phones the term Mobile Assisted Language Learning (MALL) has been coined (see Chinnery 2006). We have already mentioned projects using a whole class set of smart phones at the beginning of this chapter. If we want to make use of the full potential of those expensive modern phones for English lessons, e.g. ask for a verbally recorded homework, create a photo story or video production together with students, keep connected as a group through a social networking site or blog, have a videoconferencing session with buddies from a school abroad or work on fully blown online tutorial courses, we should make sure that we develop support programmes for the purchase of these phones however.

Mobile Assisted Language Learning In addition to the social issue there always remains the question as to what increasing internet use and thus use of servers and resources in general will do to our world. Being unsure with ourselves regarding the question of how much technology we want in lessons in order to support Intercultural Agency effectively and how much technology use is tenable for our environment, we leave it to you and trust you to get this balance right. And we also hope that this book has given you some kind of guidance.

Tasks

1. Have another look at your notes on task number 8 in chapter 9. Have they got anything in common with the challenges described in chapter 10.1? Why? / Why not?
2. Take a minute to reflect on what you have used your mobile phone for within the last 24 hours. Has the development of modern mobile devices lead you to a more casual and frequent use of your phone?
3. Talk to three different people to find out what kinds of apps they use most frequently on their phone/their computer at home. Find similarities and differences. Discuss together whether the results tell you more about current trends or about personal preferences.

4. Find someone with a mobile phone that has a touch screen and an internet connection. List at least ten apps that can be utilized for English teaching and learning.

Application	Use for English teaching and learning
..	..

5. Type in this link (http://www.w3.org/2010/Talks/0507New Delhi-KB-IH/slides.pdf) and have a look at this presentation by the W3 consortium. How does the semantic web differ from the current one and what advantages and disadvantages would it bring with it?
6. Have another look at the technological trends and the chapter on technology in education. How do the trends described help to develop students' intercultural Agency?
7. Has there been a new publication on the technological equipment of schools in Germany as yet? Search the web for a new edition of the cited publication (www.bmbf.de/publikationen, or any other publication that will give you the same kind of information) and check the numbers for
   - computers per student
   - the places where computers are situated within schools
   - number of smartboards per school (?)
   - number of digital projectors per school (percentage of schools with a digital projector (beamer)
   - frequency of use in language lessons
   - number of laptop classes (percentage of schools with laptop classes)
   - number of smartphone classes (?)
   * the categories with a (?) are not included in the publication from 2006
8. How much technology use is enough? And how much is too much? Discuss this question with at least one other person in your group.

SUGGESTED ANSWERS FOR THE TASKS

Sample Solutions

Chapter 2

2.1)
To be worked on individually

2.2)
Possible projects you could gather information about: Jenny's Story and Childnet Challenge

2.3)
For example:
- textbooks can offer a range of topics to be covered in e-mail projects
- Agree on the framework of the projects (duration, frequency of exchange, expectations of both teachers, presentation of results)
- Are students asked to document what they are learning with the help of a portfolio?
- Discuss critical or interesting aspects that may rise in the course of the project with the entire group
- Ask students to reflect on the insights they have gained

2.4)
Requires individual answers

2.5)
Possible articles: "E-learning and the development of intercultural competence" by Meei-Ling Liaw

2.6)
TESL= **T**eaching **E**nglish as **S**econd Language

Chapter 3

3.1)
Possible resources you can find here: "Getting video tasks online", "Create Image Books" or "Photo Assignments for ESL/EFL students in Second Life"

3.2)
To be worked on individually

3.3)
Possible resources you can find here: instructions on how to create audio files and RSS-feeds

3.4)
For instance, a brainstorming on the term "Cyberbullying" as a pre-viewing activity, an analysis of the cinematic devices employed to underscore the message of the film as a while-viewing activity and and a role play representing the different parties involved in the issue as a post-viewing activity

3.5)
Individual answers are required

Chapter 4

4.1)
For instance, the *New York Times* portal: the range of categories you can choose from, the limited number of resources you can access each month, the numerous videos this newspaper offers

4.2) and 4.3)
To be solved individually

4.4)
For instance

Site	BBC Learning English
Target Group	Ranges from EFL students at school to business people
Features	English in general, Business English, Grammar, Vocabulary, Pronunciation, Sport, quizzes, The Flatmates, Community, Section for Teachers, Specials, Introduction of Authors, Downloads

Comments	Pronunciation exercises are comprehensive and restricted to the southern English accent

4.5)
Individual answers are expected

4.6)
Translation suggested by Google:
Regarding an overall assessment of Mrs. M., in spite of these weaknesses to the credit that it has sought to capture the complex field of error analysis and the associated linguistic traditions of theoretical and empirical-practical applications of data on learner.

4.7)
Possible answers: translation tools are known not to be completely reliable as they can't compensate a lack of language skills

4.8)
Pick an article on an internationally significant event on www.nytimes.com , compare the US-American coverage to the one you find on comparable German newspapers and identify parallels and differences

Chapter 5

5.1)
Possible answers:
a) Google
b) Reputation, efficiency
c) Looking for something that you are not sure where exactly to find it

5.2) to 5.4)
Individual answers are expected

5.5)
For instance:
Potentials: Familiarizing students with the internet as a source of information, practicing presentation skills etc.

Limitations: Students might not stick to the relevant sites, dependence on technical equipment

5.6)
For example:
Students and teachers need to be familiar with the technical equipment/ there needs to be a plan B in case the internet at school breaks down/ the WebQuest needs to be clearly structured/ one might restrict the sites students can access to the relevant ones only

5.7)
Word: teacher education/ Consulted search engines: Google.de, Yahoo.com and Ask.com
- Wikipedia is the first hit you get with all three of them, other than that the entries are quite diverse
- Yahoo.com gets the most hits and suggests further words/ concepts related to the one you have searched for
- Google.de offers you to choose websites in German only

5.8)
You can check the spelling of words/ find the corresponding pictures to English words (e.g. patio)/ visit places like Buckingham Palace in 3-D with the help of Google Earth

5.9) and 5.10)
To be solved individually

Chapter 6

6.1)
You first of all need to get an idea of what the different kinds of activities are really aiming at, before deciding which one to work with. Once you know how to implement which activity in your English class, the creation itself is rather easy

6.2)
Diagnosis enables the teacher to cater for the different needs of individual students/

A holistic approach ought to be considered (e.g. include all of the four skills)/ it definitely is time-consuming

6.3)
To be worked on individually

6.4)
If students upload the results of tasks they had to work on, the teacher can get an idea of the knowledge they have gained in the course of the class/ the teacher can keep track of dynamics and processes of a group work if the forums are used for discussions

6.5)
One example would be the SMART © Table, which can be used during group work

6.6)
Doing a quiz with the SMART © voting system to check how much knowledge students have retained after having worked on a topic for several weeks

6.7)
Individual solutions are required

Chapter 7

7.1)
To be worked on individually

7.2)
For instance, *MasterTool 3.0 Autorensystem* in 2011

7.3)
Individual solutions are required

7.4)
This module provides, for instance, a definition of the term multimedia and an overview of its development

7.5)
The levels of competence of the CEFR range from A1, A2 and B1, B2 to C1, C2

Chapter 8

8.1)
Possible answers: privacy settings, clickjacking, reliability. All being concepts that express an increasingly critical reflection on the use of social software and media

8.2)
- A wiki can be created to display the students' results after having dealt with one topic in class for some time.
- Students might cross-check or enhance already existing wiki entries on the basis of the knowledge they have acquired in class.
- students first need to be familiarized with the formatting codes the respective resource works by

8.3)

	Wiki	Blog
Your own personal site		X
An open source data base for texts on a specific topic	X	
A collaboratively created website in English about your home town	X	X
A site that informs and provides news on a given topic		X

8.4)
- Inform students about possible measures they can take when being bullied

- Create a critical awareness of how to go about your use of social media (e.g. what information to share etc.)
- Endorse an attitude that embraces rather than discriminates against diversity

8.5)
Possible ways to integrate a podcast in your English class:
- publishing audio/video files that were created during class (e.g. when dealing with literature)
- news podcast section as part of the homepage of a school

8.6) and 8.7)
To be worked on individually

Chapter 9

9.1)
Lessons can prepare you by creating as many authentic scenarios to practise your English as possible

9.2)
English for special purposes
Content knowledge
Set phrases
Colloquial English
An idea of polite communication patterns in the respective foreign language

9.3)
The conference call can be simulated with the help of a VoIP resources like Skype

9.4)
Such e-mail projects ought to encourage students to reflect on their own and the foreign culture as much as possible, while always trying to figure out the pros and cons of what they are conveying and learning, respectively. And then prompt them to ask themselves, how come they perceive things in a specific way.

9.5)
Possible answers:
Scaffolding: division of each topic into subtopics etc.
Autonomy: Students can choose how to present results

9.6)
For example:

Computer Applica- tion	Knowledge	Skills	Awareness
Facebook	terms and conditions, netiquette	Social skills, navigating on Facebook, basic computer skills	Importance of privacy settings, visibility on the net, the perma- nent mark one leaves, who to share what information with, motives for using Facebook

9.7)
For instance: exposing the students to as much native speaker English as possible/ simulating as many authentic speaking oc- casions as possible etc.

Chapter 10

10.1)
Individual solutions based on individual answers to 8.9)

10.2)
Possible answers: checking your Facebook account on your smartphone

10.3) and 10.4)
To be worked on individually

10.5)
Possible answers:
Advantage: you start to see a connection between things that you did not know were related to each other/ a multitude of information is available at the same time
Disadvantage: loss of privacy

10.6)
Possible answers: Online communication in general (E-mail projects, Skype projects etc.) enable students to interact with English-speaking countries and thereby foster Intercultural Agency

10.7) and 10.8)
To be solved individually

Bibliography

Abbit, J., & Ophus, J.. 200). What we know about the Impacts of Web-Quests: A review of research. *AACE Journal, 16*(4),441-456.

Alby, Tom. 2008. *Web 2.0. Konzepte, Anwendungen, Technologien.* 3. Auflage. München: Carl Hanser Verlag.

Al-Seghayer, Khalid. 2001. The Effect of Multimedia Annotation Modes on L2 Vocabulary Acquisition: A Comparative Study. In: *Language Learning & Technology,* Vol. 5, No. 1, January 2001, pp. 202-232.

AVALON. 2010. *3rd Evaluation Report based on an "AVALON Post-Course-Survey"* October 2010. Found on the Internet: URL: https://files.pbworks.com/download/Ikzkiv3I26/avalonlearning/33461963/Avalon_Evaluation_Report_Post_Course_Survey.pdf (28.12.2010).

AVALON. 2009a. 1st Evaluation Report based on an "AVALON Experts' Survey" April 2009. Found on the Internet: URL: https://files.pbworks.com/download/YMHY4jUiGS/avalonlearning/33805917/Avalon_Evaluation_Report_Experts_Survey.pdf (28.12.2010)

AVALON. 2009b. 2nd Evaluation Report based on "AVALON Experts' Interviews" December 2009. Found on the Internet: URL: https://files.pbworks.com/download/Gi9nwmyPnH/avalonlearning/33811433/Avalon_Evaluation_Report_Experts_Interviews.pdf (28.12.2010).

Bax, Stephen. 2003. CALL – past, present and future. In: *System* 31,1/03, 13-28;

Belz, J. 2001. Institutional and individual dimensions of transatlantic group work in network-based language teaching. *ReCALL* 13 (2), 213-231.

Betts, J. D., & Glogoff, S. J. (2004). *Instructional models for using weblogs in e-learning: A case study from a virtual and hybrid course.* Paper presented at the Syllabus 2004 Conference, San Francisco, CA. Retrieved November 21, 2007, from http://download.101com.com/syllabus/conf/summer2004 /PDFs/w01.pdf.

Bildung+. 2010. *Second Life Education? Pro und Contra zum Lernen in der viralen Welt.* Found on the Internet: URL: http://www.bildung-plus.de/medien/sites/Second_life_education.html. (30.12.2010)

Bloch, J. (2007). Abdullah's blogging: A generation 1.5 student enters the blogosphere. *Language Learning & Technology, 11(2)*, 128–141. Retrieved March 14, 2008, from http://llt.msu.edu/vol11num2 / bloch/default.html.

Boulton, Clint. 2009. Green-minded Google Gets Red-faced Over Search Energy Consumption Claims. In: *eweek*. Found on the Internet: URL: http://www.eweek.com/c/a/Search-Engines/Green-minded-Google-Gets-Redfaced-Over-Search-Energy-Consumption-Claims/ (28.12.2010)

Bundesministerium für Bildung und Forschung. 2006. IT-Ausstattung der allgemein bildenden und berufsbildenden Schulen in Deutschland. URL: www.bmbf.de/pus/it-ausstattung_der_schulen_2006.pdf

Bryant, Todd. 2006. Using World of Warcraft and Other MMORPGs to Foster a Targeted, Social, and Cooperative Approach Toward Language Learning. In: *Academic Commons*. Found on the Internet: URL: http://www.academiccommons.org/commons/essay/bryant-MMORPGs-for-SLA

Byram, Michael. 1997. *Teaching and Assessing Intercultural Communicative Competence*. Clevedon: Multilingual Matters.

Chinnery, George M.. 2008. You've got some GALL: Google-Assisted Language Learning. In: *Language Learning & Technology*. February 2008, Volume 12, Number 1, pp. 3-11.

Cutrim Schmid, Euline (2009). *Interactive Whiteboard Technology in the Language Classroom: exploring new pedagogical opportunities*. Saarbruecken, Germany: VDM Verlag Dr. Mueller.

Dam, Leni. 2003. *Developing L earner Autonomy : The Teacher's Responsibility*. In : Little, Ridley & Ushioda (eds). *Learner Autonomy in the Foreign Language Classroom: Teacher, Learner, Curriculum and Assessment*. Dublin: Authentik, pp. 135-146.

Davies,Graham. 2010. *ICT4LT*. Found on the Internet: URL: http://www.ict4lt.org/en/index.htm (28.12.2010)

DeveloperWorks. 2006. *developerWorks Interviews: Tim Berners-Lee*. Found on the Internet: URL: http://www.ibm.com/developerworks/podcast/dwi/cm-int082206.txt. (30.12.2010).

Dodge, Bernie. 1995. *Some Thoughts About WebQuest*. Found on the Internet. URL: http://webquest.sdsu.edu/about_webquests.html. (28.12.10).

Domínguez Miguela, Antonia. 2007. *Models of Telecollaboration (3): eTwinning.* In: O'Dowd, Robert. 2007. *Online Intercultural Exchange. An Introduction for Foreign Language Teachers.* Clevedon: Multilingual Matters.

Donath, Reinhard. 2010. *Teachers' Training Web 2.0.* Found on the Internet: URL: http://donathwebzwei.wordpress.com/. (28.12.2010)

Donath, Reinhard. 2010. *Englischunterricht in der Informationsgesellschaft.* Found on the Internet: www.englisch.schule.de (28.12.2010)

Donato, Richard. 1994. *Collective Scaffolding in Second Language Learning.* In: Lantolf, J.P., Appel, G. (Eds.). *Vygotskyan Approaches to Second Language Research.* pp. 33-56. Norwood, NJ: Ablex Publishing Corporation.

Ducate, Lara, Lomicka, Lara. 2009. Podcasting: An Effective Tool for Honing Language Students' Pronunciation? In: *Language Learning & Technology*, Vol. 13, No. 3, October 2009, pp. 66-86.

Ebersbach, Anja, Glaser, Markus, Heigl, Richard. 2008. *Social Web.* Konstanz: UVK Verlagsgesellschaft.

Egan, Kieran. 2008. *The Future of Education: Reimagining Our Schools from the Ground Up.* New Haven and London: Yale University Press.

Ellermann, Carmen. 2008. Halfway around the World in 80 Clicks. Im Weblog mit einer Partnerklasse diskutieren. In: *Der fremdsprachliche Unterricht Englisch.* 96, pp. 14-19.

Giles, Jim. 2005. Internet encyclopaedias go head to head. In: *Nature* 438, 900-901.

Godwin-Jones, Robert. 2010. Emerging Technologies: New Developments in Web Browsing and Authoring. In: *Language Learning & Technology.* February 2010, Volume 14, Number 1, pp. 9-15.

Godwin-Jones, Robert. 2009. Emerging Technologies. Personal Learning Environments. In: *Language Learning & Technology*, June 2009, Volume 13, Number 2, pp. 3-9.

Grgurovic, Maja, Hegelheimer, Volker. 2007. Help Options and Multimedia Listening: Students' Use of Subtitles and the Transcript. In: *Language Learning & Technology* Vol. 11, No. 1, February 2007, pp. 45-66.

Grimm, Nancy. 2010. *Australia & New Zealand: Beyond the "Tourist Kit" Approach in the EFL Classroom.* In: Eisenmann, Maria, Grimm, Nancy & Volkmann, Laurenz. *Teaching the New English Literatures.* Heidelberg: Winter, pp. 19-24.

Hampel, Regine, Hauck, Mirjam. 2004. Towards an Effective Use of Audio Conferencing in Distance Language Courses. In: Language Learning & Technology, Vol. 8, No. 1, January 2004, pp. 66-82.

Hansen, Lauren. 2009. What happened to Second Life? In: *BBC Mobile. News.* Found on the Internet: URL: http://news.bbc.co.uk/2/hi/8367957.stm (05.01.2011)

Hewett, B. (2000). Characteristics of interactive oral and computer-mediated peer group talk and its influence on revision. *Computers and Composition, 17*(3), 265–288.

Holec, Henri. 1981. *Autonomy and Foreign Language Learning.* Oxford: Pergamon.

Hubbard, Philip. 2004. Another Look at Tutorial CALL. In: *ReCALL* 16 (2), pp. 448-461.

Kanuka, H., Rourke, L., & Laflamme, E. (2007). The influence of instructional methods on the quality of online discussion. *British Journal of Educational Technology, 38*(2), 260-271.

Kern, Richard,Warschauer, Mark. (Eds.). 2000. *Network-based Language Teaching: Concepts and Practice.* Cambridge: Cambridge University Press.

Kern, Richard, Ware, Paige, Warschauer, Mark. 2008. *Network-Based Language Teaching.* In: van Deusen, N, Hornberger, N.H. (Eds.). 2008. *Encyclopedia of Language and Education.* 2nd Edition, Volume 4: Second and Foreign Language Education, pp. 281-291.

Koo, Kyosung. 2006. Effects of using corpora and online reference tools on foreign language writing: a study of Korean learners of English as a second language. In: *Iowa Research Online.* Found on the Internet: URL: http://ir.uiowa.edu/cgi/viewcontent.cgi?article=1250&context=etd. (28.12.2010)

Kortecamp, K., & Bartoshesky, A..2003, March. *WebQuest: An instructional tool that engages adult learners, promotes higher level thinkingand deepens content knowledge.* Paper presented at the Society for Information Technology and Teacher Education International Conference 2003, Albuquerque, NM.

Kramsch, C. (1993). *Context and Culture in Language Teaching.* Oxford: Oxford University Press.

Leahy, M., & Twomey, D.. 2005. Using web design with preservice teachers as a means of creating a collaborative learning environment. *Educational Media International, 42*(2), 143-151.

March, Tom. 2003. The Learning Power of WebQuests. In: *Educational Leadership*, Volume 61, Number 4, pp. 42-47.

Maddux, C., & Cummings, R.. 2004. Fad, fashion, and the weak role of theory and research in information technology in education. *Journal of Technology and Teacher Education, 12*(4), 511-533.

Milson, A.J.. 2002. The internet and inquiry learning: Integrating medium and method in a sixth grade social studies classroom. *Theory and Research in Social Education, 30*(3), 330-353.

Molebash, P., Dodge, B., Bell, R., & Mason, C.. 2002. *Promoting student inquiry: WebQuests to web inquiry projects (WIPs)*. Paper presented at the Society for Information Technology and Teacher Education International Conference 2002, Nashville, TN.

Möllering, Martina, Ritter, Markus. 2007. *Computer-mediated Communication: Its Potential for Language Acquisition and Intercultural Learning*. In: Zhang, F. / B. Barber (eds.). *Handbook of Research on Computer-enhanced Language Acquisition and Learning* Melbourne: Melbourne University Press)

Müller-Hartmann, Andreas. 2000. The role of tasks in promoting intercultural learning in electronic learning networks. *Language Learning & Technology* 4 (2), 129-147. On the internet: URL: http://llt.msu.edu/vol4num2/muller/default.html.

Müller-Hartmann, Andreas, Schocker-von Ditfurth, Marita. 2004. *Introduction to English Language Teaching*. Stuttgart: Klett.

Müller-Hartmann, Andreas, Schocker-von Ditfurth, Marita. 2011. *Teaching English: Task-supported language learning*. Paderborn: Schöningh.

Müller-Hartmann, Andreas, Raith, Thomas. 2009. Web 2.0. Das Mitmach-Internet für den Fremdsprachenunterricht nutzen. In: *Der Fremdsprachliche Unterricht Englisch* 96, pp. 2-7.

Murphy, Philip. 2007. Reading Comprehension Exercises Online: The Effects of Feedback, Proficiency and Interaction. In: *Language Learning & Technology* Vol. 11; No. 3, October 2007, pp. 107-129.

Murray, J.H.. 1997. *Hamlet on the Holodeck: The Future of Narrative in Cyberspace*. New York: The Free Press.

Murray, R.. 2006. WebQuests celebrate 10 years: Have they delivered? *Action Research Exchange*, 5(1).

Nandorf, Katja. 2004. *Selbstlernen mit Sprachlernsoftware. Multimedia in der fremdsprachlichen Weiterbildung*. Tübingen: Narr.

Nardi, Bonnie A., Ly, Stella, Harris, Justin. 2007. *Learning Conversation in World of Warcraft*. Found on the internet. URL: http://www.artifex.org/~bonnie/pdf/Nardi-HICSS.pdf. (28.12.2010)

O'Dowd, Robert. 2007. *Online Intercultural Exchange. An Introduction for Foreign Language Teachers*. Clevedon: Multilingual Matters.

O'Dowd, Robert, Ritter, Markus. 2006. Understanding and Working with 'Failed Communication' in Telecollaborative Exchanges. In: Calico Journal, Vol. 23, pp. 623-642.

O'Dowd, Robert, Ware, Page. 2009. Critical Issues in Telecollaborative Task Design. In: *CALL Journal*, Vol. 22, No. 2, April 2009, pp. 173–188.

O'Rourke, Breffni. 2007. *Models of Telecollaboration (1): eTandem*. In: O'Dowd, Robert. 2007. *Online Intercultural Exchange. An Introduction for Foreign Language Teachers*. Clevedon: Multilingual Matters.

Pilkington, Doris. 1996. *Rabbit proof fence. The true Story of one of the Greatest Escapes of all Times*. New York: Harper Collins.

Richards, Cameron. 2005. The Design of Effective ICT-Supported Learning Activities: Exemplary Models, Changing Requirements, and New Possibilities. In: *Language Learning & Technology*. Vol. 9, No. 1, January 2005, pp. 60-79.

Richardson, Will. 2009. *Blogs, Wikis, Podcasts, and Other Powerful Web Tools for Classrooms*. Thousand Oaks: Corwin Press.

Ritter, Markus. 1995. *Computer und handlungsorientierter Unterricht. Zur allgemeinen und fremdsprachendidaktischen Reichweite eines neuen Mediums*, Auer: Donauwörth

Ritter, Markus. 2007. *Zum Stellenwert digitaler Medien im fremdsprachlichen Klassenzimmer*. In: Müller-Hartmann, A./M. Schocker-von Ditfurth (eds). *Proceedings des VIII. Mediendidaktischen Kolloquiums*, Heidelberg 2006. Frankfurt: Lang Verlag.

Robb, T. 2003. Google as a quick 'n dirty corpus tool. In: *TESL-EJ*, 7(2). Found on the Internet: URL: http://www-writing.berkeley.edu/TESl-EJ/ej26/int.html. Questgarden. 2010. *Quest Garden. Where the great WebQuests grow*. Found on the Internet: URL: http://questgarden.com/. (28.12.2010)

Robb, T. 2003. Google as a Quick 'n Dirty Corpus Tool. In: *TESL-EJ On the Internet*. Vol 7, No. 2. Found on the internet: URL: www.tesl-ej.org/wordpress/volume7/ej26/ej26int/ (03. September 2010)

Rüschoff, Bernd, Wolff, Dieter. 1999. *Fremdsprachenlernen in der Wissensgesellschaft*. Ismaning: Hueber.

Rüschoff, Bernd. 2008. *Output-Oriented Language Learning With Digital Media*. In: Thomas, M.. *Handbook of Research on Web 2.0 and Second Language Learning*. Hershey, PA: IGI Global USA, 42-59.

Schmidt, Torben. 2007. *Gemeinsames Lernen mit Selbstlernsoftware im Englischunterricht – Eine empirische Analyse lernprogrammgestützter Partnerarbeitsphasen im Unterricht der Klasse 7*. Tübingen: Narr.

Stern.de. 2007. *Wikipedia schlägt Brockhaus*. Found on the Internet: URL: http://www.stern.de/digital/online/stern-test-wikipedia-schlaegt-brockhaus-604423.html (05.01.2011)

Suárez García, Jesus. 2007. *Models of Telecollaboration (2): Cultura*. In: O'Dowd, Robert. 2007. *Online Intercultural Exchange. An Introduction for Foreign Language Teachers*. Clevedon: Multilingual Matters.

Sun, Yu-Chih. 2009. VOICE BLOG: AN EXPLORATORY STUDY OF LANGUAGE LEARNING. In: *Language Learning & Technology*, June 2009, Volume 14, Number 2, pp. 88-103.

Sharma, Pete, Barrett, Barney. 2007. *Blended Learning: Using Technology in and Beyond the Language Classroom*. Oxford: Macmillan.

Steffen, Angelika. 2009. Selbstmarketing – Mit Xing und Twitter Karriere machen. In: *Fokus Online*. Found on the Internet: URL: http://www.focus.de/finanzen/karriere/berufsleben/tid-15059/selbstmarketing-mit-xing-und-twitter-karriere-machen_aid_422304.html (28.12.2010)

Swarup, Vikas. 2008. *Slumdog Millionaire*. New York: Scribner.

Thaler, Engelbert. 2008. *Teaching English Literature*. Paderborn: Schöningh Verlag.

Trinder, Ruth. 2006. *Language Learning with Computers: The Students' Perspective: A Theoretical and Empirical Investigation*. Frankfurt am Main: Lang.

Tsai, S.. 2006. *Integrating WebQuest learning into EFL instruction*. Paper presented at the Society for Information Technology and Teacher Education International Conference 2006, Orlando, FL.

Ushioda, Ema. 2003. *Motivation as a socially mediated process*. In: Little, Ridley & Ushioda (eds). *Learner Autonomy in the Foreign*

Language Classroom: Teacher, Learner, Curriculum and Assessment. Dublin: Authentik, pp.90-102.

Ushioda, E.. 1996. *Learner Autonomy 5: The Role of Motivation.* Dublin: Authentik.

Van Lier, Leo. 2010. *Foreword: Agency, Self and Identity in Language Learning.* In: O'Rourke, Breffni, Carson, Lorna (Eds.). 2010. *Contemporary Studies in Descriptive Linguistics, Vol. 3. Language Learner Autonomy. Policy, Curriculum, Classroom.* Frankfurt am Main: Peter Lang.

Volle, Lisa M.. 2005. Analyzing Oral Skills in Voice E-Mail and Online Interviews. In: *Language Learning & Technology,* Vol. 9, No. 3, September 2005, pp. 146-163.

Vygotskij, Lev S. 1973. *Thought and Language.* Cambridge, Mass.: M.I.T. Press.

Warschauer, M. .2004. Technological change and the future of CALL. In S. Fotos & C. Brown (Eds.). *New Perspectives on CALL for Second and Foreign Language Classrooms* (pp. 15-25). Mahwah, NJ: Lawrence Erlbaum Associates.

Waschk, Katja. 2008. *Öffnung des Englischunterrichts in der Grundschule. Studien zur Wahlfreiheit und Lernerautonomie.* Duisburg: Universitätsverlag Rhein Ruhr.

Willis, Jane, Willis, Dave. 2007. *Doing Task-based Teaching.* Oxford: Oxford University Press.

Wood, D., Bruner, J., & Ross, G. (1976). The role of tutoring in problem solving. *Journal of child psychology and psychiatry,* 17, 89-100.

World Wide Web Consortium (W3C). 2010. *W3C Semantic Web Activity.* Found on the Internet: URL: http://www.w3.org/2001/sw/ (28.12.2010)

INDEX

A

Asynchronous oral communication **37-39**
Asynchronous written communication 23
Audio conferencing **36**, **37**, 40
Authoring software **97-99**
Autonomy 13, **180-183**
AVALON Project 159, **167**, **168**

B

Behaviouristic CALL 14, 15
Blackboard 107-109
Blogosphere 145
Blogs (weblogs) **145-151**, 170
Bulletin boards **27**, 32

C

CALL computer assisted language learning 11-17
CEFR Common European Framework of Reference 131
Chat 21-23
CMC computer mediated communication 15, **30**, **31**
Communicative CALL 14
Concordancing programme/concordance 60-63
Corpora 60-63
Critical media literacy 183-185
Cultura 24
Cyberbullying 44, **152-154**

D

Data Driven Learning 14
Determinist view of technology use 188
Diagnostic tools 96, **100-107**
Digita 128, 138
Discussion boards 27, **39**
Drill-and-practice 15

E

e-mail projects 24-27
e-portfolio 105, 106
e-Tandems 24
eTwinning 25

F

Forums 27

G

Google 64, **81-85**

I

ICC Intercultural Communicative Competence (Byram) 176-180
Iceberg model of culture 179
ILIAS 109
Information age 15
Instrumental view of technology use 184
Integrated CALL 16
Intercultural agency 174-176
IWB games 116, **118-122**
IWB interactive slate 115
IWB interactive whiteboards 112-115
IWB voting system 115-117

K

Key pal exchanges 24
Laptop classes 194
LMS learning management systems **107-109**, 195

M

MALL Mobile Assisted Language Learning 196
Mash ups 193
Microblogs 151, 152
Moodle 28, **107-111**
MUVE Multi User Virtual Environments 156-161

N

NBLT network based language teaching 11
Net safety 89, 90
Netiquette **152**, 170
Network society 192
Normalization of CALL 16

O

Online dictionaries 58, 59
Online encyclopaedias 66, 67

P

PBL Project Based Learning 85
PDA Personal Digital Assistants 191
Personal profiles 145
Podcasting 38, **154-155**
PVE Personal Virtual Environment 191-192

R

Reference tools 58-67
RSS Feeds 86, 87

S
Scaffolding 181-183
Scanning 85
Search engines 81-90
Search engines for kids 89, 90
Second Life 156-161
Skimming 85
Smart phones 15, 191, 196
Social bookmarking sites 87, 88
Social networking sites
Social software 15, **142-161**
Speech recognition 131, 132
Sustainable technology use 194
Synchronous oral communication **21**, **22**, 36
Synchronous written communication 21, 22

T
TBL Task Based Learning 159
Technological developments /trends 190-193
TELL technology-enhanced language learning 11
Textbook-independent software 131-134

Textbook-related software 127-131
Thesaurus 60
Translation tools 63-65
Tutorial courseware 56, **126-134**

V
Video conferencing 36, 37
Video messaging 38, 39
Voice blogs 167
Voicemail 37

W
W3 Consortium 193
Web 2.0 142-161
Web portals 49-58
Web vs. Internet 48, 49
WebQuests **74-81**, 158
Wikipedia 66, 67
Wikis 142-144
World of Warcraft 185
WYSIWYG What you see is what you get 143